What O

MW00365486

"Sarah Hamaker writes with keen understanding about sibling rivalry, a problem that vexes many of today's parents. Sarah shows how parents can aggravate sibling conflict—and also provides the solutions to having a more harmonious home. *Ending Sibling Rivalry* solves the problem of sibling conflict by addressing the core issues. It's refreshing to find a book that tackles a much-needed topic with a common sense and practical approach."

—John Rosemond, family psychologist,
nationally syndicated columnist, and author,
The Well-Behaved Child,
Parent Babble

"*Ending Sibling Rivalry: Moving Your Kids from War to Peace* is a must have for any parent of multiple kids. Author Sarah Hamaker skillfully weaves the best practices of everyday parents from across the country into a manual that is biblically based and time tested. The volume is full of ideas and practical tips that is sure to enhance the quality of life (and peace) for every family that practices its suggestions. Addressing the age-old issue of sibling rivalry is no longer taboo as Sarah presents a positive, encouraging plan for growing the unique personality of each of your children while teaching him/her valuable life lessons of teamwork, conflict resolution, appreciation, and God's plan for family."

—Patti Garibay, National Executive Director and founder,
American Heritage Girls, Inc.

"Sibling squabbles are an issue all parents with multiple children wrestle with. Sarah gives a refreshing perspective on how to handle and view sibling rivalry. Rather than just focusing on the fight of the moment, she encourages us to keep the bigger picture in mind—that 'sibling conflict is the first class in relationship training.' So true. This book offers practical advice that leads to positive, lifelong implications in the world of family and relationships."

—Jean Blackmer, author,
Boysterous Living: Celebrating Your Loud and Rowdy Life with Sons
MomSense: A Common-Sense Guide to Confident Mothering

"Any family that has more than one child needs this book! Sarah Hamaker has done a remarkable job providing practical, biblical, and well-researched solutions for one of the greatest challenges for all families: sibling conflict. This book contains a wealth of strategies and will be a treasure for all who read it."

—Dr. Scott Turansky, co-founder,
National Center for Biblical Parenting

"In *Ending Sibling Rivalry*, Sarah Hamaker provides a new roadmap to family harmony—but one based on age-old wisdom. Don't be surprised if in this easy, enjoyable read, Sarah takes you from harried to hopeful when it comes to facing the sibling rivalry in your own family."

—Betsy Hart, syndicated columnist and author,
It Takes a Parent

Ending Sibling Rivalry

Blessings on your
parenting journey!
Sarah Hawk

ENDING Sibling RIVALRY

MOVING YOUR KIDS FROM WAR TO PEACE

SARAH HAMAKER

BEACON HILL PRESS
OF KANSAS CITY

Beacon Hill Press of Kansas City
PO Box 419527
Kansas City, MO 64141
www.BeaconHillBooks.com

ISBN 978-0-8341-3364-8

Printed in the
United States of America

Cover Design: Ryan Deo

Library of Congress Cataloging-in-Publication Data

Hamaker, Sarah.
  Ending sibling rivalry : moving your kids from war to peace / Sarah Hamaker.
    pages cm
  Includes bibliographical references.
  ISBN 978-0-8341-3364-8 (pbk.)
  1. Jealousy—Religious aspects—Christianity. 2. Sibling rivalry. 3. Brothers and sisters—Religious aspects—Christianity. I. Title.
  BV4627.J43H36 2014
  248.8'45—dc23

                                                    2014021474

The Internet addresses, email addresses, and phone numbers in this book are accurate at the time of publication. They are provided as a resource. Beacon Hill Press of Kansas City does not endorse them or vouch for their content or permanence.

10 9 8 7 6 5 4 3 2 1

Contents

Acknowledgments

I'm grateful for the assistance many provided in the shaping and writing of this book. At the top of the list is my husband, Christian, and four children (Naomi, Leah, Micah, and Silas). Their encouragement and willingness to help carve out additional writing time for me was invaluable to my finishing the book on time. I offer sincere thanks to the dozens of parents who shared their stories of sibling rivalry with me and allowed me to provide a glimpse of those stories in my book. Many friends and family provided much-needed moral support during the writing process.

"Brothers and sisters are as
close as hands and feet."

—Vietnamese Proverb

Introduction

From our downstairs office, I could hear a ruckus upstairs—screams that didn't sound like shouts of joy. With four children between the ages of five and eleven, I'd grown used to a certain amount of loudness, but my maternal radar detected something different in these outbursts.

I followed the source to my girls' room, where Naomi was attempting to drag Leah, her younger sister, out of the room because Naomi "wanted to be alone." Never mind that the room was both of theirs: Naomi wanted to be by herself. Thinking that an eleven-year-old was a little too young to pull a Greta Garbo routine, I separated the pair for a cooling-off period.

Ah, the joys and trials of parenting multiple children! Sometimes we view children in the plural as little people who add to a family's stress and tension, instead of bringing more joy and love. If you say you have three, four, five, or more kids, strangers, acquaintances, friends, and sometimes even relatives comment on how chaotic your household must be, how tired you as a parent must get, how tight your finances must become, and how anxious about paying for college you must be. What these and similar comments show is how as a society we've changed our expectations of child-rearing—that raising children is so difficult that fewer kids makes things easier for all involved.

In reality, being a sibling isn't unusual. Estimates indicate around 80 percent of people have brothers or sisters. What has changed in the last half century is the average family size. United States fertility rates reveal that large families used to be the norm in this country. In 1800, the total U.S. fertility rate was 7.04 children per woman, according to the U.S. Census Bureau. By 1850, that number had dropped to 5.42, before falling even further to 3.56 in 1900. The U.S. fertility rate continued to decline throughout the first half of the twentieth century before rising briefly to 3.53 in 1960 (the baby boom generation). The rate bottomed out at 1.77 in 1980, then slowly rose before leveling out early in the twenty-first century. The U.S. Census Bureau puts the total U.S. fertility rate at 1.88 children for 2012, below the 2009 rate of 2.05 and under the replacement fertility rate of around 2.1.

Those statistics underscore that the desired family size has fluctuated over the years. In the United States, the typical early-nineteenth-century woman birthed between seven and ten children. The Gallup organization, which has gathered data on what Americans deem as their ideal family size since 1936, reported that up until 1957, the majority of Americans wanted families with three or more kids. The number of kids per family dropped between 1957 and 1978 to an average of about 2.5 children, around where it hovers today.

A mere decade later, more women began having only two children, which meant the number of women having more than three children dropped. Census data shows that in 1976, 59 percent of women between the ages of forty and forty-four had three or more kids. Three decades later, the percentage of women in that age-group with three or more children had decreased to 28 percent. Nowadays, in the United States, two children per family has become the number-one choice, with 52 percent of adults surveyed by Gallup in 2007 saying that two kids were the ideal number. Part of the switch to smaller family sizes can be attributed to the fact that more children live to adulthood in twenty-first-century America than in the not-so-distant past. As recently as 1900, a U.S.-born baby had only a 50 percent chance to reach adulthood.

Contributing to family size is that more families now consist of two working parents than in the past. In general, larger families have slipped out of general favor. Adding to that is the fact that more American women between the ages of eighteen and thirty-four are opting to have a single child. (In 1985, the U.S. Census reported that figure at 12.7 percent. Around 2010, that had inched up to 13.9 percent of women between the ages of eighteen and thirty-four only wanting one child.)

As our ideal family size has shrunk, our view of how children should be raised has become more complicated—and with that, the expectations of how children should behave toward one another. By all accounts, families with multiple children are experiencing more sibling rivalry than in the past. Parents are frustrated and concerned about the battles that erupt on a frequent—even daily or hourly—basis in their homes.

In my own research for this book, I interviewed and surveyed more than sixty families with more than one child on how their offspring interacted with one another—and how the parents felt about the hostilities. What these parents told me echoes what other parents have posted in online forums, talked about at the bus stop, and worried about among friends. From my sibling rivalry survey, here are some of the common responses to sibling conflict and concerns about how that fighting impacts sibling and family relationships.

- "Mostly, my kids fight because they don't see the needs of their siblings as important as their own," said Angela Vermilion of Aldie, Virginia. "They can be very others-centered and have big hearts for those outside the family, but very selfish when it comes to siblings."

- "I'm concerned that my kids' fighting disrupts everyone around them," said Brandi Dixon of Birmingham, Alabama, of her four children.
- "I do worry that as adults, they won't be close if they continue to not get along," said Ruth Reid of Dade City, Florida.
- "It troubles me because the root of the problem is usually an unaddressed sin area," added Colleen Scott of Marysville, Ohio.
- For Tracie[1] of Sterling, Virginia, "the pettiness of the fighting" bothered her the most. "I wanted them to learn to fight fair and resolve the conflict so that the same things didn't keep coming up," she said.
- Humphrey Mar of Vienna, Virginia, struggled with how immature the conflicts were. "It's just not that big of a deal what they're fighting over," he said.
- The whipsaw emotions of the sibling relationship—"The fact that they are sometimes tight as can be one moment and so cruel the next"—triggered distress in Meghan of Arlington, Virginia.
- Michelle Boice of Manassas, Virginia, found herself dealing with siblings who tried to parent and the hard feelings that ensued. "They sometimes assumed parenting roles, like reminding each other to do something they should be doing or not to do something that may get them into trouble. Then the other one gets irritated that their sibling is telling them what to do," she said.
- "I find myself trying to ensure that the older doesn't railroad the younger because she's smarter or stronger, while the younger ones don't get their way by appealing to par-

ents to solve all of their problems," said Dan Schantz of Powhatan, Virginia.

What these comments illustrate is that many parents struggle with the inevitable fights and disagreements of their children. No parents want sibling rivalry to rule their households, but many are flummoxed as to how to stop it. As Jane Mersky Leder asks in her book *Brothers & Sisters: How They Shape Our Lives,* "Who said sibling rivalry was inevitable, anyway?"[2] Yes, sibling conflict does exist—and it does occur in every family. But Americans especially have become obsessed with sibling rivalry, with many parents simply accepting that it's normal for their children to fight all the time.

In a *Psychology Today* article on the subject, Leder pointed back to Sigmund Freud as starting the whole mess with his theory that all brothers and sisters compete with each other for the love and attention of Mom and Dad. "It's colored our perception of sibship ever since. Therapists and lay people alike tend to view the relationship largely as one of struggle and controversy," she wrote. "And family experts have underemphasized the sibling relationship, instead concentrating on parents and children and husband and wives. Small wonder that sibling rivalry is accepted as the normal state of affairs."[3]

Even with fewer siblings around in most families, that familial relationship has more of an impact on kids than previously considered. Parents instinctively know that the relationship of siblings has an important role in the development of their children, a fact supported by recent scholarship on this connection. Since the early 2000s, all manner of experts—anthropologists, biologists, psychologists, sociologists, and even zoologists—have started seriously looking into the relationships of brothers and sisters. Areas of study include the genetic, sociological, and psychological aspects. Research has found that by the time a child reaches the age of eleven, he has spent around 33 percent of his free time with his brothers and/or sisters. That's much more time than with friends, teachers, parents, or alone, according to a 1996 Penn State University study.[4] A 2005 study found that even teens choose to hang out with siblings around ten hours a week—more time than previously thought.[5]

Given those statistics, it's not surprising that siblings rank near the top of who sways kids the most. But all that togetherness can spill over into sibling squabbles. Studies by psychologist Laurie Kramer with the University of Illinois's Family Resiliency Center showed that, on average, three- to seven-year-old siblings engaged in conflict—a sustained, hostile exchange—once every seventeen minutes.[6] Studies like these fuel the perception that siblings are constantly at each other's throats, and that it's normal for kids to fight so much.

While sibling conflict is part of the brother and sister relationship, it doesn't have to wreck your children's interactions in the short term or long term. We don't have to wait for the inevitable friction with fear and trepidation. We can—indeed, we should—guide our children toward sibling harmony, knowing that while conflict will come, the strong bonds of love and family will help them weather those storms. As parents, we don't have to take on the full duty of making our kids get along—we need to shift the bulk of that accountability where it belongs, on the shoulders of our children.

"Back when I thought it was my responsibility to ensure friendship and peace in the home, I worried that they would drift away from one another or hurt their relationships in the long term, or that they would learn and reinforce their own bad patterns that would carry on to other relationships," said Deb Elkink of Elkwater, Alberta.

Siblings leave a legacy for each other, one that informs all aspects of our lives. As Frank Bruni wrote in "The Gift of Siblings" in the *New York Times*, "I sometimes wonder, when it comes to the decline in fertility rates in our country and other [nations], whether the economic impact will be any more significant than the intimate one. For better or worse, fewer people will know the challenges and comforts of a sprawling clan."[7]

This book will provide guidance on how you can put your kids on the path from enemies to friends. We'll look behind the scenes to how parents can contribute to sibling rivalry, as well as give ways to mitigate potential conflict. We'll also focus on the positive aspects of siblings—the blessings and the skills kids learn through brother-and-sister interactions. Now as we embark on this journey toward sibling harmony in your household, the way may seem steep and the steps impossible to navigate safely, but the rewards of a calmer, less chaotic home and happier children await you and your family at the end.

"Sibling relationships—and 80 percent
of Americans have at least one—
outlast marriages, survive the death
of parents, resurface after quarrels
that would sink any friendship.
They flourish in a thousand incarnations
of closeness and distance, warmth,
loyalty and distrust."
—Erica E. Goode

The Importance of Getting Along

My arrival eleven years after her birth pushed my sister Shawn from the position of youngest in our family. That transition may—or may not—have contributed to the infamous egg-on-the-slide incident. When I was four years old, my mother left me in the care of Shawn. We had a metal swing set in the backyard, and I begged Shawn to get a piece of waxed paper to sit on and slide down "fast as lightning." Shawn went inside for the waxed paper but came out instead with a raw egg.

Lobbing the egg with perfect precision, she timed its descent to coincide with my arrival at the end of the slide. Splat! I shot off the slide like a bullet, landing hard on the ground, covered in egg goop. To this day, Shawn insists that she was "only trying to help me go fast" down the slide, but no one believes her.

Many brothers and sisters have similar stories of conflict, which has been a hallmark of sibling relationships since the beginning of time. Biblical examples of brother and sister fights abound. Cain killed Abel because he was jealous that God accepted Abel's offering and not his, that Abel was first in God's eyes. Jacob wanted to be the firstborn, and so he tricked his twin, Esau, out of his birthright. Sisters Leah and Rachel had their share of disagreements over their husband, Jacob. His father's favoritism of Joseph triggered jealousy and hatred in Joseph's brothers.

Literature also has numerous instances of sibling rivalry. It's no surprise that Shakespeare frequently turned to sibling conflict in his plays. *King Lear* shows the father provoking his three daughters to compete for his love, while sisters Bianca and Kate fight constantly in *The Taming of the Shrew*. *As You Like It* has two sets of siblings in contention with each other: Oliver and Orlando, and Duke Senior and Duke Frederick.

Many famous real-life siblings have had public conflicts. The Andrews Sisters—that powerhouse singing trio of LaVerne, Patty, and Maxene of the 1930s and '40s—played nice onstage but clashed loudly offstage. Twins Ann Landers and Abigail Van Buren—dueling advice columnists for many years—had a relationship that waxed and waned in terms of rivalry for most of their adult lives.

As these examples show, sibling rivalry can cause lasting rifts that destroy relationships. The ripple effect of unresolved sibling conflict goes beyond the brothers and sisters directly involved in the fight to the rest of their family and even friends too.

Setting the Spark

The term "sibling rivalry" didn't become part of the child-rearing vocabulary until the twentieth century. Child psychiatrist David Levy coined—and then popularized—the term in the 1930s following a series of experiments that supposedly exposed the aggression of siblings toward each other.[1] Levy followed in Sigmund Freud's footsteps in positing that brother and sister animosity was part of every sibling relationship.

What most parents fail to realize is that while conflict between brothers and sisters is inevitable, the interaction between siblings doesn't have to become a rivalry. Siblings fight for a variety of reasons; each family has its own list because each family dynamic is different. But there are some general causes as to why siblings fight with each other, and understanding the rationale can help parents look beyond the conflict to solutions.

In an informal survey of parents with multiple children that I conducted, the number-one instigators of sibling fights were toys and possessions, followed by being teased and jealousy. Wanting parental attention rounded out the top four reasons. "My number-one concern is that sibling conflict will leave a lasting mark," said Meghan of Arlington, Virginia. "I worry most about the middle child, who is often lambasted by her older brother."

Most articles and books on siblings and sibling rivalry list similar reasons why kids fight, but at the core of it all is a desire to be number one and to be first in all things, whether it's getting dessert or getting to the car. This is innate in all children because it's at the core of our own sinfulness: the selfishness of *me*. Generally, everyone has a selfishness problem, and that selfishness comes out in a variety of ways, including siblings who have a hard time not fighting. Sibling rivalry, if left unchecked, can infiltrate the family unit. If not addressed, sibling rivalry can weaken the family as a whole.

Getting Along

Why should parents care that their children are fighting? Jeffrey Kluger summed it up in his 2011 book, *The Sibling Effect: What the Bonds Among Brothers and Sisters Reveal About Us*:

A household with multiple siblings is a parliament of personalities that are forever in motion—and often in conflict. . . . But it can be an educational one, too: Adulthood, after all, is practically defined by peer relationships—the workplace, the marriage, the community group. As siblings, we may fight and sulk and fume, but by nighttime, we still return to the same twin beds in the same shared room.[2]

Kluger's point underscores that being pleasant and kind to one another has a more far-reaching significance than peace at that moment. Children who learn to resolve conflict within a family through interactions with brothers and sisters have an advantage when they encounter discord outside of the home.

Parents also should realize that their actions can play a role in sibling rivalry. Delving a bit deeper into the story of Jacob and Esau brings to light just how influential parents can be with sibling conflict. From their childhood, the two brothers never got along, and their animosity triggered some of the most tragic stories in the Bible: Esau selling his birthright (Genesis 25:29-34) and Jacob tricking his father for Esau's blessing (Genesis 27). The brothers parted company in anger (Esau) and fear (Jacob), and the two stayed estranged for many years.

Their parents both were culpable of hindering—instead of helping—the relationship between the twins. Genesis 25:27-28 shows how Isaac and Rebekah's favoritism and their failure to teach the boys to get along soured their sons' interactions: "When the boys grew up, Esau was a skillful hunter, a man of the field, while Jacob was a quiet man, dwelling in tents. Isaac loved Esau because he ate of his game, but Rebekah loved Jacob."

That also points to the most important reason why parents should assist their children in moving from sibling rivals to friends: They will not be children long, and the things learned—or not learned—in childhood can have a long reach into adulthood. Carolyn Greene of Powhatan, Virginia, shared that her son and daughter became close in childhood, a state that has continued into adulthood.

"I like to think they got along so well because, when they were very young and rivalries broke out between them, I sat them in chairs facing each other and asked them to tell the other the best thing they liked about them," said Carolyn. "Obviously, as young children, they had trouble articulating, so I prompted them with things like, 'Remember the time you told me [something good] about [sibling]?' That child would nod in agreement, and the other seemed surprised and pleased to hear such positive statements. It only took about three times, but those short sessions changed and strengthened the dynamics between them that has lasted the rest of their lives."

As Carolyn's story illustrates, the significance of siblings being friends more than enemies involves more than a surface calm for your household. There are some lasting benefits to nixing sibling rivalry among your offspring. Here are some reasons why getting along with brothers and sisters is so important.

Lasting friendship. Most parents know that their children won't be kids for long, but what many of them fail to consider is that what happens in childhood can have an impact into adulthood. One theme about sibling fighting that kept popping up among parents I talked with was the fear that conflict in childhood would lead to estrangement when the children grow up. "I'm concerned that the fighting of my three elementary-school-age children will create a distance between them that will last into adulthood," said Ashley Turner of Birmingham, Alabama.

❏ ❏ ❏

PARENTAL VISION

From large to small, successful companies are the ones that have a mission statement or vision for the future. All policies, procedures, and strategic goals are centered around fulfilling that vision. Parents who develop a vision for their children will find it helps their day-to-day decisions as well as their future planning. Coming up with such a "parental vision" for your kids is fairly easy. (Parental vision was originally proposed by family psychologist John Rosemond in several columns and books and is used here with permission.)

Simply write down the answer to the following question: If someone asked you to describe each of your children at age thirty, what would you say?

It's practically guaranteed that hardly anyone reading this book wrote down one or more of the following:

- Graduated at the top of his high school or college class
- Went to an Ivy League school
- Played a professional sport
- Has a fancy house
- Has a high-paying job

Instead, most parents would jot down things like the following:

- Compassionate
- Godly
- Hardworking
- Honest
- Kind
- Loving
- Respectful
- Responsible
- Thoughtful
- Truthful

When comparing the two lists, you'll notice that the first one is all about achievements—status symbols and the like that mark a person's "place" in this world. The second list is all about characteristics, what makes a man or woman underneath the outer trappings of material things. If what you really want for your children is for them to become good, upstanding citizens, then you will need to raise them with these characteristics in mind.

Talk with your spouse about your parental vision for each of your children at age thirty. Write down your list and post it someplace where you can reference it on a regular basis. Think about what's on the list; then, ask yourself if your decisions as a parent reflect the vision you have for your kids. How do the things you encourage your children to accomplish build toward the vision you have for them as adults?

Now whenever you wonder what to do about discipline, consequences, addressing behavior, or virtually any parental decision, think about that vision. For example, if your child shirks his chores, remember that you want him to be hardworking and responsible. That should assist you in correcting his behavior. If your child is mean to her sibling, keep in mind you want her to grow up to be loving—and then act accordingly.

When you have a clear vision for your children, your parenting decisions will become easier. Taking the long-term view of raising kids will help you in the short term. Having a vision for your kids and keeping that vision in mind as you parent will get you over both the rough and smooth patches of child-rearing.

That's why parents should raise their children with an eye to how they want these kids to be at age thirty. Develop a parental vision for your child as an adult, and make your parenting decisions with that in mind. This is especially applicable when it comes to handling sibling rivalry. If you want your children to be friends later in life—or at least cordial to each other across the table at holiday meals—then pay attention now to sibling conflict.

Tiffany Amber Stockton, mother of two preschoolers in Colorado Springs, Colorado, put it this way: "What troubles me most when they fight is that they won't realize what potential exists for them to be great friends and will continue with the animosity."

Conflict resolution. "I see sibling fights as the place where they first learn about conflict," said Betsy DeMarco, a mother of two boys and two girls in Fairfax, Virginia. Knowing how to resolve the inevitable conflicts that we come across in our lifetimes can be one of the best gifts we can give our kids. Learning the ins and outs of negotiation, peacemaking, and diffusing anger are skills that will be well used. (Chapter 7 will cover in detail how to teach conflict resolution to kids.)

What concerns Elaine Carilli of Columbia, South Carolina, the most when her six children between the ages of two and fourteen squabble is "that they will never be able to get along, resolve conflict, live in peace, and love each other." She makes it a point to help her children get along by using Scripture to teach them what the Bible says about loving one another and how much God loves us. "I emphasize that love and how it calls us to put others before ourselves," she said.

A preserving spirit. Sometimes, a brother or sister won't readily give in to the request (or demand) of a sibling. The asking party often will regroup and try again until a more satisfactory outcome is achieved—or until he realizes his sibling isn't going to budge. Siblings also push each other to finish tasks, learn something new, or excel at a sport.

In our house, my four children cajole and press each other to figure out things like riding a bike without training wheels, climbing the monkey bars, and tying shoes. This type of interaction also shows how much the siblings care about one another. Whether it's by not giving assistance when begged or by shouting encouragement on the spot, brothers and sisters can be just the impetus kids need to achieve their goal.

Wordplay. Who doesn't recall a brother or sister saying something mean to you or having just the right word at the right time? Julie Arduini of Youngstown, Ohio, doesn't want her two children to "use words that tear the other down," when fighting. While that old nursery rhyme about words not hurting is catchy, we all have had experiences where the power of words cut us deeply.

That's why what we don't allow our children to say—and what we do encourage them to say—has more consequences than we might think. (We'll discuss this more in subsequent chapters.) As children learn to get along with siblings, they also can develop the skills to use words wisely. Parents play a crucial role in helping children bridle their tongues when it comes to their brothers and sisters—and others they come in contact with as well.

All about me. By encouraging our kids to get along, we're also reminding them to think of others before themselves. "We are all self-centered," said Jennifer Coffin, a Fairfax, Virginia, mother of three grown children. While that focus on self is something we all spend a lifetime overcoming, we should remember that selfishness is often at the center of sibling rivalry.

Part of our job as parents is to show our children how to think of others. (Chapter 2 will explore more fully how to teach this concept to our children.) "I don't want my children to consider themselves more important than their siblings," added Lelia Jones, a mother of three elementary-school-age children in Columbia, South Carolina. She asks them to think about how they can love their siblings that day, such as fixing drinks or food for one another.

Open hands. Siblings who learn to live in harmony also have mostly mastered the art of sharing. This doesn't mean automatically giving in to the other's requests for toys or attention, but that we should say yes more than we say no.

In our house, we stress how being generous with our things and time is a way of blessing others. For example, I remind my older girls that reading to their younger brothers when asked is a small way to show their love. This doesn't mean a child has to share a toy or time every time a sibling asks, but we should gently remind our children of how being less territorial with our things and time is honoring to God. (Chapter 9 covers this topic in more detail.)

A Strong Bond

The more your children get along in childhood, the deeper their relationships will be in adulthood. That's not to say that brothers and sisters who fought all through high school are doomed to have a terrible relationship in college and beyond—there is hope that those more contentious interactions will become calmer later in life. However, as parents, we have a duty to give our children the tools they need to become responsible adults—ones with whom we will want to spend time.

When our children are young, we must be willing to guide them to have an appreciation for each other, to resolve conflict in a positive and uplifting manner, to have an open heart for their siblings, and to build each other up rather than tear each other down.

Sibling conflict is the first class a child receives in relationship training. If a parent emphasizes honor and other virtues in family life, such as serving others, valuing others, and listening to others' opinions, then sibling interactions are likely to change for the better. While no family will ever be entirely free from conflict, we can have a home without sibling rivalry.

"Sometimes being a brother is even
better than being a superhero."

—Marc Brown

Thinking the Best, Not the Worst

On my daughter Leah's ninth birthday, her older sister gave her a gift. Now in some families, this wouldn't have been remarkable, but since our children generally didn't exchange presents, it was. Not only was the present unusual in itself, but its contents were even more so, because Naomi had given her younger sister perhaps the best gift of all.

Leah had been saving for more than a year for an American Girl doll. We had told both girls that if they saved half of the doll's price—a fairly large sum of money for girls who only received around a dollar a week for allowance—we would kick in the other half (a one-time deal!). Naomi, being older and thus receiving more allowance, achieved her goal six months earlier. On her birthday, Leah had a mere two dollars left to go.

When Leah unwrapped her sister's gift, there sitting on the table were eight quarters in two neat stacks, the exact amount she needed to buy her doll. Needless to say, it was quite the gift of generosity and was beautiful to behold.

Similar acts of charity should be frequent in our homes, but in reality our children rarely perform such magnanimous deeds for each other. Why do our kids treat one another with meanness instead of kindness, with a shove rather than a helping hand, and with harsh words instead of a sweet spirit? Because of their own sinful hearts, yes, but also because we have failed to instill in them how to truly love one another.

"In today's world, there is entirely too much focus on self, and it is a daily struggle to instead turn our hearts away from self," wrote Judy Barrett in her self-titled blog on "How to Raise Children with a Servant's Heart." "I want them to have a love and a heart for others. . . . I hope by instilling this value in my children when they are young, that they will be better equipped as adults to think of others first."[1]

Watchful Eyes

Before we dive into the suggestions on how to teach children to think well of each other, parents should first take the pulse of their household. Observing kids when they think no one is looking can be eye-opening. The dynamics of their interplay can appear differently when grownups step back and stealthily pay close attention to them. Cheryl Harnden of McLean, Virginia, practices this in her home. "I praise them for getting along and 'catch' them being good by getting along," she said, adding that she sometimes tells them "how happy it makes me when they play well together." Mary in Owego, New York, also keeps an eye out for such commendable actions. "I notice and praise when one of them does something nice for the other," she said.

Sometimes, we get caught up in the moments—the crazy morning rush out the door, the after-school info and paper dump, the dinnertime tango, the activities and homework and bedtime routines all jumble together to create time-pressed and chaotic days. All of that busyness can make us miss the interactions between our kids, either good or bad. Those distractions also can make us focus only on the negative exchanges because those are the ones that interrupt schedules or frazzle nerves at the end of a long day.

To check the barometer of your household, take a week to watch your children with your full attention. How your children treat each other when no one is looking says a lot about how rife sibling rivalry is in your household. As you observe from a distance, ask yourself these questions:

- Do your kids share easily with each other *most of the time?*
- Do your kids talk kindly to each other *most of the time?*
- Do your children help each other without being asked *most of the time?*
- Do your children play together or spend time together voluntarily *most of the time?*
- Do your children do nice things for one another without parental prompting *most of the time?*
- Do your children defend each other to outsiders *most of the time?*

Note the qualifier *most of the time.* Everyone can have a bad day—that's why you should observe at least several days to gather enough intelligence to make a good assessment. Remember that you shouldn't expect perfection or altruism in every single interaction between your offspring. Instead, use these questions to help you consider your children's overall behavior toward one another.

Before you're discouraged by how little your children cooperate with each other, remember that children aren't born with an innate ability to serve others. That skill needs to be consciously developed, preferably beginning at a young age. Don't despair if your children are older or even grown—there's still time for you to point them in the right direction.

Warm Fuzzies

If you think well of someone, you aren't as quick to pick a fight, shove him aside for that last piece of cake, or call him names, right? That doesn't mean you always treat him perfectly, but warm feelings will hamper your impulse to be not so nice. The same is true of our children, albeit in a more undeveloped form. If they can acquire a deep abiding love and care for their siblings, then they will be less likely to continue in destructive behaviors toward them.

Think about families with children who truly appear to like each other's company. How do they treat each other? Do they put each other down? Do they make snide remarks about their siblings to others? Do they seem to want to be with each other? Do they appear happy together? If you ask parents of those children, I'm sure they would tell you that their children fight sometimes—it would be very unrealistic to expect conflict never happens—but that the fights are usually of short duration and that the children kiss and make up quickly.

Those families have discovered that helping children develop—and cherish—a kind and generous relationship with each other is the foundation for healthy sibling interactions. This training should start as soon as your child begins to understand words and their meanings. A toddler is too immature to realize the importance of being kind to siblings, but not too young to be taught how to be nice. "One of the toughest things to teach a child is how to do for others in a selfless manner," said Barrett on her blog. "Toddlers almost instinctively take toys away from each other and one of the first words they learn is usually, 'Mine!', even though this is rarely said in most households."[2]

That instinctive coveting of toys has to be tempered with a spirit of giving—and no toddler will learn that lesson entirely on her own. While the reflexive nature of toddlers is to grab for themselves, the good news is that they also enjoy helping others if prodded in the right direction. As your child grows, you should become more deliberate in teaching her how to give and how to serve her family—and eventually the church, community, and the world at large.

This rest of this chapter will focus on concrete ways to teach your children to become siblings who have a servant's heart toward each other. No matter the age of your children, there are some general principles parents can follow when setting the stage for your kids to think well of each other. Not all of these suggestions will be appropriate for your family at this time, nor will every family execute these ideas perfectly. The key is to be intentional in focusing on your child's heart toward his siblings because starting with the right heart attitude can make all the difference in reducing conflict.

One final word of caution: if the following proposals haven't been implemented in your family before now, don't try to tackle them all at once! Pick two or three that you think will have the most chance of immediate success and work on integrating those into the fabric of your family life. When you think your offspring have mastered those, start adding others along the way. As long as you are trying to develop a household of family members that uplift one another, you will be on the right track. Also, you'll want to adjust and expand—or contract—these suggestions as your kids grow. Some will be better suited for elementary-school-age kids, while others might work well with teenagers. You know your family best, so use your judgment on which ideas to implement and which to leave on the page for now.

The Inner Child

As Christians, we should have a care toward developing our child's inner self, his heart, and conscience. "It's my responsibility to teach my kids ways to be kind," said Jennifer Coffin of Fairfax, Virginia. She added that she and her husband made this education an integral part of their children's upbringing, following the example of the apostle Paul, who reminds us in Galatians 5:13-15 that we are called to put our freedom in Christ to good use: "For you were called to freedom, brothers. Only do not use your freedom as an opportunity for the flesh, but through love serve one another. For the whole law is fulfilled in one word: 'You shall love your neighbor as yourself.' But if you bite and devour one another, watch out that you are not consumed by one another." To assist in this preparation, here are some ideas on how to mold the heart to think of others.

Pray. As believers, this is the first place to start. We should petition God for our children daily in our private communication with our Lord, but we should not neglect family prayers on their behalf as well. This can help all members of the family to see their importance before God, their parents, and siblings. Both private and public prayers should enlist the Lord to strengthen the family harmony and cultivate a servant's heart toward one another.

Family prayer time can uplift and unify. Having kids share requests, hear answers to prayers, and even pray for one another goes a long way toward treating each other well. "I've constantly prayed in thankfulness to God in their hearing for each of their siblings," said Brandi Dixon, mother of four young kids in Birmingham, Alabama. A family that sincerely and regularly prays together will be more apt to have the others' best interests at heart.

Start with love. It might seem overly simplistic, but encouraging your children to express love to their siblings is a good place to begin fostering deliberate care for one another. Just saying "I love you" can be a powerful diffuser of tension and can remind children of the family bond they share with each other. As the child matures, you can show him how to add to that sentiment. "I try to have times where we say what we love about each other, especially at the end of a long day of fighting," said Angela Vermilion of Aldie, Virginia. This usually can go a long way toward mending the hurts caused by unkindness.

In God's image. One of the most basic ways to cultivate a charitable attitude toward each other is "to enforce that each of them is created in God's image," said Russ, a father of four in Pittsburgh, Pennsylvania. Pointing our children to Christ can remind them of the example Jesus has given us in how to treat one another. For instance, when a child remarks on something a sibling has done (maybe his sister wouldn't share a toy or his brother made a snide comment to him) remind the child that both he and his sibling were made in the image of God, that we all reflect God in some way.

This also can temper jealousy and envy that can occur because of a sibling's appearance, talents, or abilities. If we talk to a complaining child—"But Suzy's hair is curly and mine is straight, and I really want curls!"—about how God made her just right and in his holy and perfect image, we can reorient feelings that lead to uncharitable actions and thoughts.

Our family. God created the family unit in Genesis 2:24: "Therefore a man shall leave his father and his mother and hold fast to his wife, and they shall become one flesh." Reminding our children of this foundational truth—that they are part of this family for God's good purpose—can help reinforce the idea that all members of the family need to stick together through thick and thin, and even sibling conflict. Elizabeth Spencer of Battle Creek, Michigan, regularly preaches the "we are a family. . . . We mourn and rejoice with one another" sermon to her two daughters to reinforce this truth.

Perfect placement. The idea that each child has her own special place in the family goes along with the family being put together by God. Some disagreements stem from a child wanting to have a different place in the family. Maybe she sees her older brother as "having all the fun." Maybe she's the oldest and resents her little sister, "getting away with murder." Wherever the child is in the sibling birth order, emphasizing to her that she is loved exactly as she is could help alleviate those negative feelings. Also talking about the privileges and benefits to being the oldest, middle, or youngest—and there are pros and cons to each position—would remind her of how well she fits into that place.

Teach the Golden Rule. The concept of treating others as you would like to be treated has taken a beating in today's all-about-me culture. Many kids have never fully grasped what the Golden Rule looks like in practice. Don't let your kids miss out on this vital concept, one that if learned and practiced regularly will be a guiding principle throughout their lives.

Start by having them memorize Matthew 7:12 ("So whatever you wish that others would do to you, do also to them") or Luke 6:31 ("And as you wish that others would do to you, do so to them"). Then unpack the verses to uncover their meaning and how that applies to their lives. Work from the basic idea of treating others like you want to be treated. Have discussions as to how that would play out in a variety of scenarios. Play the "what if" game with older kids, such as "What if such-and-such happened? How would the Golden Rule apply to that situation?" Those debates can help flesh out the concept that the other person matters (and matters more than our own desires and wants). Discuss how we should behave toward one another—an essential component to grasp if one is to grow a strong servant's heart.

Memorize Scripture. As the psalmist wrote in 119:11, "I have stored up your word in my heart, that I might not sin against you." Hiding God's Word in our hearts is a fantastic way to guard against sin of all kinds. Another plus is that the Holy Spirit uses Scripture to convict our hearts and bring to mind pertinent passages on treating each other well, especially when we're not being obedient to the Word. The Spirit's work can stem the tide of bad feelings and turn a potential dustup into a mere whisper. The Bible abounds with verses that address the issue of treating each other well. Have the entire family commit those passages to memory.

Our family picked Ephesians 4:32 as one of our "kindness" reminders: "Be kind to one another, tenderhearted, forgiving one another, as God in Christ forgave you." When a child starts to say unkind things about a sibling, I prompt her to quote this Bible verse. If two children are squabbling, I often ask both of them to repeat the verse. Saying the Word of God aloud has shortened many a fight as the children turn their eyes off themselves and onto Jesus.

Here are a few more applicable passages that address the topic of kindness toward one another that would be wonderful additions to your Scripture memorization library:

- "Rejoice with those who rejoice, weep with those who weep. Live in harmony with one another. Do not be haughty, but associate with the lowly. Never be wise in your own sight" (Romans 12:15-16).
- "For you were called to freedom, brothers. Only do not use your freedom as an opportunity for the flesh, but through love serve one another. For the whole law is fulfilled in one word: 'You shall love your neighbor as yourself'" (Galatians 5:13-14).
- "Finally, all of you, have unity of mind, sympathy, brotherly love, a tender heart, and a humble mind" (1 Peter 3:8).
- "And let us consider how to stir up one another to love and good works" (Hebrews 10:24).

Some families choose to focus on a passage of Scripture dealing with a topic with which the group as a whole is struggling. "For one whole school year, we worked on memorizing Philippians 2:1-8," said Alice of Vienna, Virginia. "Then we discussed a lot the idea of what it meant to put others' interests ahead of our own." When you start with the Word of God as your foundation, the rest of your building grows much stronger.

Spoken Words

Once the innermost heart of the child has been addressed, it's time to start with the outward manifestations of servanthood. What we say has a great impact on our hearers. Uplifting words make us happy, while snappy words can sour our mood in a heartbeat. Helping children to understand the power of words is essential to their behavior toward each other becoming more servant-like.

Speak well of all. It can be expedient to express our exasperation or frustration about one child to another, especially if a spouse is not around as a sounding board. But we need to restrain that impulse because it can create tension between the siblings and also unwittingly spark rivalry. "As a single mom, it's often tempting to complain to one about the other's behavior," said Mary, a mother of two teens in Owego, New York. "But I have to avoid this because it just gives them ammo when they fight." The children should follow that rule as well, and not bad-mouth each other to a third party (sibling or friend, for example), especially not behind someone's back.

Beyond not complaining about one child in another's hearing, parents should be deliberate in building up their children to each other. Cindy Damon of Fairfax, Virginia, speaks positively about her two young children's relationship and what good friends they are to them and to others. "We also provide positive experiences for them to have together, to cement that relationship further," she said. Amy of Baltimore, Maryland, also follows that advice with her children. "When they do something good, I'll say that while our family is together for all to hear," she said.

Watch the language. One of the most destructive things in any relationship is name-calling. Calling someone names that are derogatory, disparaging, belittling, deprecating, derisive, and ridiculing tears apart the relationship. Most such instances happen in the heat of the moment, and the damage can last long after the sincerest apology has been delivered. If you think back to your own childhood, I'm sure you can still recall the sting of those names uttered long ago. Allowing our children to speak so disrespectfully of their siblings poisons their connection. Left unchecked, that poison will gradually erode any good feelings between them, leaving their bond in tatters.

We should try to make our home places where name-calling is taboo. Yes, all children will call a brother or sister "stupid," "dummy," and other hurtful names when vexed, angry, or bored, but we must establish a zero-tolerance policy in regard to name-calling. "When our four kids were young, we didn't allow sarcasm or put-down speech," said Jane Thompson of Sarasota, Florida. She kept a tight rein on such nasty words to avoid harming the sibling tie.

Some families might insist that name-calling is only kids joking around, but keep in mind Jesus' words in Matthew 12:34b: "For out of the abundance of the heart the mouth speaks." Proverbs 4:23 puts it this way: "Keep your heart with all vigilance, for from it flow the springs of life." As parents, we cannot let sarcastic, name-calling speech flow from our children's mouths without correction or it will destroy their relationship and breed contempt, among other nasty feelings that can fester into a very messy—and very large—problem. Nip destructive speech in the bud. You won't be able to eliminate it entirely, but you can and should be able to create an atmosphere of kindness instead of seething anger.

No teasing. Taunting, while not strictly name-calling, is its kissing cousin as far as its destructive nature. Teasing by siblings causes a fairly large part of the fighting among brothers and sisters. According to my informal sibling rivalry survey, 43 percent of the fights between siblings were triggered by teasing. In fact, being teased by a brother or sister was the second-most cited reason that fights started among the children. Sibling teasing also was by far the biggest impetus of fights parents who took the survey recalled having with their own siblings.

Discourage interactions that verge on being mean, belittling, or otherwise putting down the other person—or her actions and abilities. Be careful not to take general roughhousing or interplay between siblings as teasing—no need to go overboard on what is most likely kids being kids. However, if you suspect one child is being picked on, then keep an eye on that child. If you see a fairly clear pattern of lots of tears or avoidance of the other child (or a combination of the two), then you might need to step in and correct the problem. Take care not to assign a victim/villain role to the children, as this can exacerbate sibling rivalry. (See chapter 7 for more on victims and villains.)

Say something nice. The old adage, "If you can't say something nice, don't say anything at all" can be helpful in keeping hurtful speech at bay, but rarely do we see the flip side—that our speech should be peppered with niceties. Children often have no idea how to say something nice to another person, especially when that person shares a room with them.

Prompt your children to recall good things about their sibling relationships, such as pointing out how a brother picked up all the toys the night before or a sister, on her own initiative, read a book to the child. Make it a practice to have everyone— parents included—say something nice about a family member on a regular basis, such as around the dinner table or on Sunday afternoons. Sure, the kids will likely start with silly things like, "I like your shirt," but as you continue—and if you ban repeats—the compliments will grow more sincere and expansive. Karen in Milford, Delaware, often asks her two children to say three things about their siblings "that are cool. It boosts the opposing child's view of himself and brings them together more."

Compliments also have a way of bridging the distance between two warring siblings. In Janet Marney's Fairfax, Virginia, home, anytime one of her sons came to complain about his brother, she asked him to first say something complimentary about the sibling. "We emphasized saying and talking nice things about each other, and that helped them treat each other better," she said. The bonus was that by prefacing the complaint with compliments, often the complainer didn't get around to what had brought him to his mom in the first place.

Embrace the differences. This might seem like a no-brainer. Of course, we know our kids are not exactly alike, but don't we allow ourselves the experience of treating them essentially the same? We should take the time to be deliberate in talking about our kids as individuals to their siblings. "We try to highlight the ways our two children are different and praise them for those areas where they are gifted and in the things they aren't good at but try to be so," said Cathy Martin of Ashland, Nebraska. "That way, everyone has a wonderful contribution to the whole family."

Also, use opportunities to remind a child of his sibling's goodness to him, especially when that child is smarting over something the sibling did. Deb Elkink of Elkwater, Alberta, pointed out the areas of excellence and special skills or talents each child had to the others. "For example, I would say, 'Yes, it was wrong of him to take your toy away and I disciplined him. But remember that he shared his candy with you yesterday,'" she said. That can help move the hurting child to healing, and restore the sibling relationship faster.

Apologize when necessary. The art of apologizing has become something of a joke in society these days. Politicians and celebrities, among others, often give "non-apology" apologies, not quite admitting any wrongdoing and not really appearing contrite for the act itself. Instead, their "I'm sorry" acquires a going-through-the-motions sheen, leaving hearers unsatisfied and vaguely unsettled. That is not the kind of apology that mends fences and heals wounds. "I'm sorry" needs to be more than mere air because apologizing can be—nay, should be—a powerful way to communicate how you view the other person. In chapter 7, we will cover the steps to apologizing in more detail, as it is an integral part of conflict resolution.

Check motivation. It's human nature to attribute to ourselves noble intentions for our words and actions, but the reality is usually far from respectable. Since children are still developing their consciences, we must prod them to be introspective when it comes to the source of their actions.

You can help make your children aware of their own reasons for not thinking well of each other by engaging them in conversation about the incident. Sometimes, it's best to wait until tempers have cooled in order to gain maximum impact, but you can connect with the child in real time too. "We call this 'charitable judgment,'" said Humphrey Mar of Vienna, Virginia. "We tell our three children to check their motivation in talking about your sibling. We say, 'Ask yourself if you're just being a tattletale.'" Other questions to ask include:

- What did you hope to gain?
- What did you think you would lose?

Keep in mind that you shouldn't grill your kids for every misbehavior toward a sibling because that can be ineffective and frustrating for both you and the child. Instead, do motivation spot checks from time to time to help keep everyone on the right path.

The Siblings

Ever notice that the most successful sports teams spend a lot of time building camaraderie? The coaches understand that a team with ties beyond their team membership is more likely to work together in harmony and have less divisive strife. The same is true of families. Does your family feel like a team or like a group of individuals residing under the same roof?

If you have a group and not a team, then it's time to work on constructing a more cohesive family unit. Think about the sports teams analogy and how they accomplish this. They work hard together on a regular basis toward a common goal. This can be achieved in the family through shared chores, projects, and outings. All you need to do is to create opportunities for your kids to work together. Lucy Morgan-Jones of Boort, Victoria, Australia, gives her four children chores to accomplish together. "It builds team spirit," she said.

However, have a care that you don't turn team-building into a competition. (See chapter 3 for more information on how to eliminate unhealthy competition in your household.) Use the exercises listed in this section judiciously and make sure you interject enough fun to make the bonding a positive experience. Sure, your kids might be closer if they paint the entire house together one summer, but they also might have fonder memories if you interspersed that chore with a trip to a local water park and other fun activities. "We give them a job to do, such as protect the younger sibling or ask the older ones to be a role model," said Cheri S. of Battle Creek, Michigan.

Don't forget to have opportunities for the entire family to work on a project together too. In my family, the six of us have raked leaves and stained the deck together, as well as decorated the Christmas tree and visited the library. All of those things knit us closer together as we build shared memories. Here are a few more ways to build a cohesive team of siblings.

Walk in their shoes. When you take the time to stop and put yourself in someone else's point of view, it can be eye-opening in more ways than one. "I think it's good practice for them to consider the other child's situation," said Cathy Martin in Ashland, Nebraska. "I think when they see the other child's perspective, they naturally want to do good because they really do love each other."

This also goes hand-in-hand with the Golden Rule. Having a child try to imagine what the other sibling is feeling is a powerful way to encourage empathy. "Help the child understand the *why* of the other one's position or anger," said Tracie in Sterling, Virginia. "We taught our two children to step into the other person's shoes and see the conflict through the other's eyes."

You can use examples from outside the family to make this point too. When a child recounts a story about a friend (positive or negative), ask how the child thinks the friend felt. When reading a story or book, talk about how a main or secondary character might have felt during a conflict. When a child complains about a classmate's behavior, guide the child to view the incident from the other's point of view. We often use this tactic when a child comments on something that happened at school. For example, one child repeatedly told stories of a particular classmate who continually got into trouble. Rather than letting my child dwell on the wrongdoing, as kids often do, I reminded the child that not every home looked like ours, that perhaps something happened at home that morning that put the child in a bad mood. Use such language to draw your child's attention to the possibilities of differences in upbringing, home life, family situations, and so forth, that can bring understanding of the classmate. Then you can gently bring up similar thoughts when a brother or sister vexes the child to bring that principle home.

Put family first. Service should begin at home, to paraphrase an old English saying ("Charity should begin at home"). Children who learn to serve others in their family will be better equipped to take that attitude into the world away from home. Sometimes, we can get so focused on serving those outside our families that we forget this important lesson.

When a child does some act of service for a sibling, it can help him to view that brother or sister in a more positive light. Simple ways kids can serve the family include planning birthday parties for their siblings, shopping for holiday gifts for family members, attending important events for their siblings, and offering tea and sympathy to a sick brother or sister. "We made sure we attended family celebrations together, and went to one another's games and concerts," said Betsey Kodat of Herndon, Virginia. She also had her two daughters think about ways to help each other. "That's part of learning to do good, asking questions like, 'What do you need today? How can we help?'" she said.

Dorothy Bond-Dittmer of Akron, Ohio, made sure each of her three grown children had a special birthday all of his or her own as a child. "The other siblings' job is to help prepare and assist with the birthday party planning and execution," she said. "My daughter has mentioned many times since she has grown that she always enjoyed the other birthdays more than her own because of the participation."

In our home, I request assistance from my children in preparation and decorations for family events. For example, I tasked my oldest daughter, Naomi, with creating games for her little brother's birthday party. She thoroughly enjoyed drawing the dinosaur for "Pin the Tail on the Dino," among other game preparations. Micah was thrilled that his much-adored older sister took so much time and care just to make sure he had a fabulous party.

Focus on the outside. Join together as a family to help those outside the home. Providing frequent opportunities to serve others is a great antidote to selfishness, which is at the root of nearly all sibling conflict. Ideas include volunteering at a local food bank, adopting a World Vision or Compassion International child, visiting elderly shut-ins, and helping out at church—the possibilities are endless. One family I know drops by a nursing home each Sunday evening to talk with residents. The mother told me that at first her five daughters weren't that excited about the prospect, but now the entire family looks forward to the weekly visits. Don't forget to ask your kids for suggestions on what the family should do. You might be pleasantly surprised by how creative and how excited they are to make a difference in their communities.

The Parents

Mothers and fathers have their own responsibility to help their children grow a servant's heart. Our influence is generally the first our kids are exposed to, and studies have shown parental persuasion has a lasting impact on children. Here are some additional ways we can lead by demonstrating the principles discussed in this chapter.

Set the example. How you treat your own brothers and sisters sends a powerful message to your kids. While you might have unresolved issues with your siblings stemming from your childhood or beyond, settle those problems if at all possible. Of course, if that's not realistic, share with your children the basic outline of why you don't interact with your siblings.

Your own sibling relationships can serve as an example to your children of the many joys that having brothers and sisters can bring. (See chapter 6 for how siblings are a blessing.) My three much-older siblings share such a delight in each other's company. I've always enjoyed hearing them reminisce about their childhood capers because the stories clearly show their affection for one another. Yes, they've had their ups and downs as all siblings do, but that strong bond shines through and has become stronger as they grow older.

No matter what your current relationship is, determine to say only good or positive things about your siblings. "I speak highly of my siblings, and I encourage my kids to do the same," said Meghan, a mom with three kids in Arlington, Virginia. Also, make it a priority to remember their birthdays and other milestones (weddings, births, and personal achievements). We shouldn't allow ourselves to neglect our own siblings because that could send a subtle message to our children that brothers and sisters aren't important enough to keep in touch.

Make them wait. The merits of delayed gratification have filled numerous other books, so we'll only mention it briefly here. Waiting can directly tie into a servant heart. By helping our children wait their turn, not to push ahead, and to let others go first, we give them tangible ways to become more like servants. Look for opportunities to temper their tendency to be number one.

Jennifer Coffin purposefully practiced this with her three children. "If one grabs and wants things first all of the time, I made him give the object to his siblings," she said. That helped the child curb the impulse to be first and turned his eyes off himself to his siblings. In this, we should set the example by not needing to be first or to get the best. As our children watch our own attitude toward waiting our turn for things, they see Mom and Dad executing patience. That can help them practice patience and not always need to be first.

Ask for assistance. Your children need opportunities to practice servant-like behavior. Provide numerous occasions throughout the day for your kids to serve you—even if the child will take ten times longer than you to do the task and even if you might have to redo it later. For instance, with toddlers, you can tell your little one to bring you things, like diapers, tissues, and pillows. Moderate her desire to take by directing her gently to share. Show her how to be gentle with babies and kids by demonstrating the proper way to stroke a cat or touch an infant's feet. Praise her enthusiasm when she dusts instead of criticizing her performance. Give her age-appropriate tasks around the house, such as carrying wastepaper basket bags to the outside trash can, picking up toys, and wiping the kitchen floor. Enforce boundaries by physically separating her from her siblings' projects or toys. Include her when possible on family volunteer opportunities and household chores.

□ □ □

SERVANTHOOD SNAPSHOT

The Scenario: Your teenage children—two boys and a girl—have been teasing each other mercilessly. Their banter starts out light and funny but soon digresses into mean-spirited verbal punches. You want to restore their interactions to a more loving and caring place. What can you do?

The Solution: Try a "teasing fine" coupled with a "blessings jar." Decorate two mason jars, one with the words "teasing fine jar" and one with the words "blessings jar." For the "blessings jar," cut slips of blank paper and put the paper and pens in a basket next to the jar. Then gather the children together to explain the new "game." For every time one teases another—no matter how benign the words or intent—that sibling must pay a dollar into the "teasing fine jar." Then all siblings involved—the teaser and the teasee—must take a slip of paper and write down something they like about their siblings. Fold the paper and put it into the "blessings jar." When the "blessings jar" has a good amount of paper, bring it to the table after dinner and pass it around for everyone to pull out a slip of paper and read the blessing.

These two ideas—tying teasing with a fine as well as writing down something they like about the sibling—should eventually greatly reduce the teasing and encourage more loving interactions between the siblings.

❑ ❑ ❑

As she grows into a preschooler, be more deliberate in teaching her the basic principles of servanthood and the Golden Rule along with the ABCs. Follow up in elementary school with more concrete examples and suggestions, then transition into the teen years with family discussions and more active participation to foster these relationships.

These types of examples should go beyond chores. If a child could do the task, make it a point to tell her to do it. For example, I sometimes ask my older children to read to their younger siblings before bedtime. Now, I'm pleasantly surprised when the older ones will offer without prompting to read to their siblings. When I had a tight deadline for writing this book, all of my children stepped up to handle additional things so that I could spend more time working. My oldest two helped the younger two with bedtime routines, while the younger ones worked hard on not interrupting me while I was writing. This type of pulling together for a common cause firms the sibling bonds and builds a stronger team.

Show the way. It might seem elementary, but kids learn best when words *and* actions are used to teach. How you react when faced with things not going your way says a lot about your heart. Our own actions in the face of the unexpected and unwelcome teach our children how they should act. To encourage a kinder and gentler approach, we should model such a manner.

"I show my teenagers how I think well of them and others, and let them know how important it is to uplift someone instead of knock them down," said Michelle Boice of Manassas, Virginia. She also tries to build the self-confidence of her son and daughter "so they don't need to feel better about themselves by knocking someone down and that they will feel good about themselves when they lift each other up."

Finally, as we parent with the future in mind, remember that siblings are for life. Find parents you admire in your church, neighborhood, or community who have grown children and ask them about their children's relationships. As mentioned earlier in this book, siblings are the ones who are in our lives the longest. The bonds forged in childhood often blossom in adulthood, growing into warm, wonderful friendships. Remind your children that brothers and sisters are not a transient part of their lives.

Janice Fink, a Bruceton Mills, West Virginia, mother of four grown daughters, stressed this when her kids were at home. "I told them many times that friends come and go, but sisters are forever and that's why they needed to treat each other right," she said. Her diligence paid off, as her daughters enjoy closeness as adults with families of their own.

It's that reminder we should keep top of mind as we raise our kids. If we can teach them how to be an integral part of each other's lives as adults, we will have accomplished a wonderful thing. Equipping them in childhood with the tools to treat each other well is a major step toward achieving that goal. While I was researching this book, numerous moms and dads of adult children expressed to me the joy of watching their children enjoy one another's company as adults. Without a doubt, that blessing made all the hard work of raising them seem well worth the effort.

"Our siblings. They resemble us just enough to make all their differences confusing, and no matter what we choose to make of this, we are cast in relation to them our whole lives long."

—Susan Scarf Merrell

Competition

Sibling competition has been around as long as there have been siblings. Rivalry marred the relationship of the very first sibling pair, Cain and Abel, as Genesis 4:3-7 shows:

> In the course of time Cain brought to the LORD an offering of the fruit of the ground, and Abel also brought of the firstborn of his flock and of their fat portions. And the LORD had regard for Abel and his offering, but for Cain and his offering, he had no regard. So Cain was very angry, and his face fell. The LORD said to Cain, "Why are you angry, and why has your face fallen? If you do well, will you not be accepted? And if you do not do well, sin is crouching at the door. Its desire is for you, but you must rule over it."

Cain's reaction seems to indicate that he viewed the offerings to the Lord as a competition between himself and Abel. Cain's disappointment at God's rejection of his offering triggered his anger toward Abel, whose offering had been accepted by God. Cain refused to heed the words of the Lord to guard his heart against sin. That refusal led to the first murder when Cain killed his brother. Competition among siblings can have a similar devastating effect.

Competition often begins as soon as a new sibling arrives at the home. The new, often younger, sibling wants what the older sibling has, while the older sibling wants the younger sibling to go away and leave him—and his belongings—alone. (Chapter 10 will discuss ways to mitigate competition when introducing a new child to the family unit whether by birth, adoption, or remarriage.)

However, not all competition between siblings is unhealthy. For example, my two boys love racing each other to the bus stop, timing each other with stopwatches, and devising multiple games that pit them against each other. This type of friendly competition, wherein both parties are enjoying the sport and are being kind to one another while playing, is an example of how "competition" can be fun and fruitful between siblings. In my informal parenting survey, 55 percent of respondents said there was no harmful competition among brothers and sisters. But all too often, such competition is the exception and not the rule, and many families experience sibling competition as something fraught with anger, disappointment, and frustration.

Forty-five percent of respondents to my sibling rivalry survey said their children were competitive with each other, which means that many families at some point encounter some harmful competition between brothers and sisters. The competition discussed in this chapter is the kind that erodes sibling unity and feeds sibling rivalry. However, there are ways to lessen the potential harmful effects competition can have on siblings. Let's start with how competition can creep into the family, then consider how parents can help reduce competition in the home.

Competitive Beginnings

If you read any books about child-rearing and/or sibling rivalry, you'll find that most child psychologists and parenting experts contend that competition among siblings is merely their way of vying for parental affection and love. Twenty-one percent of parents in my informal sibling rivalry survey picked "wanting parental attention" as the main reason their kids fought.

But in attributing competition among brothers and sisters to merely an unvoiced or perhaps unconscious desire for parental love is to miss the larger, more harmful reason for these contests: our innate desire to have our own wants and needs fulfilled first. As discussed in earlier chapters, this selfish nature is rooted in wanting to be the best or number one, which means much of sibling rivalry takes place because of comparison or competition.

Some parents further complicate the issue by insisting that competition in the home is good practice for kids because it can prepare them for living in a dog-eat-dog world. Others view competition as a way to get ahead in life, to become a "winner" instead of a "loser." "They shouldn't have to compete for attention," said Amy of Baltimore, Maryland. "They should be valued, and then they will value others." Again, what these views fail to consider is that pitting children against one another does little to build them up into responsible and respectful adults. (The "Parental Vision" section in chapter 2 clarifies how we should raise our kids with character in mind.) While both views have a grain of truth, overall, our homes should strive to be less competitive and more cooperative, less focused on winning and more centered on respecting and loving each other. Parents should take care not to embroil their children in competition. As Maggie Ellwood of Portland, Oregon, put it: "I don't pit my kids against each other."

Lest you think it's impossible for siblings not to be involved in personal competition, here are three examples of famous sibling pairs who have found ways to eliminate personal rivalries while engaging in professional challenges in their chosen fields. Radio personalities Tom and Ray Magliozzi—known professionally as Click and Clack, the Tappet Brothers—regaled audiences for thirty-five years as hosts of National Public Radio's *Car Talk* program. Their gentle teasing and on-air ribbing endeared them to listeners almost as much as their car diagnostics. The two brothers contend their relationship off the air was much like their cordial and warm on-air banter indicated.[1]

Brothers Jim and John Harbaugh coach opposing National Football League teams. At Super Bowl XLVII in 2013, the Baltimore Ravens with head coach John Harbaugh trounced the San Francisco 49ers with head coach Jim Harbaugh to win the game. When the two brothers met on the field after the game ended, John reportedly told his younger brother how much he loved him, while Jim congratulated his brother on the victory. By all accounts, the two brothers continue to have a good relationship despite their on-field rivalry.

Tennis players and sisters Venus and Serena Williams have a fierce competitive relationship on the court, but a close, loving one off the court. A 2013 documentary of the pair showed the sisters as very different but extremely tight-knit even though they've often competed directly against each other, including in eight Grand Slam tournaments. If these siblings can leave the competition to game time, we, too, should be able to help our children stop the endless loop to be on the "winning" side.

Who Are You?

Even before our children are born, we wonder what they will be like. Will they resemble family members? Will they have similar traits? When having a second or third child, we might speculate on how the child's birth order will impact his personality. All this speculation sometimes leads to our putting labels on our offspring, but labels are one of the easiest mistakes into which parents can fall. All parents have the urge to put their children into neat little boxes—the smart one, the funny one, the creative one, or the athletic one. Even if we never consciously say the words aloud, these labels often are heard and understood loud and clear by our children.

However, labels, while appearing benign or even cute, can stir up competition and resentment among siblings. Being known for something can drive a child to succeed, usually in what he's been labeled. Another child might forgo trying to do well in an area "owned" by a sibling. In the former instance, competition heats up as each child campaigns hard in a war of one-upmanship. If Suzie the scholar brings home an A for a science project, then Billy the athlete better score a goal for his soccer team to stay in the race. When Walter the creative lands the lead in a school play, Julia the socializer feels compelled to win the student council election at all costs. Family time becomes enmeshed in a constant battle to see who comes out on top by excelling the most in their "chosen" field—then the "game" begins anew with the next event.

On the other side, the non-athletically labeled child forgoes any team or individual sport because she doesn't want to compete with her talented athletic sister. The non-academic sibling cruises through school without trying advanced placement classes to avoid not measuring up to his brainy brother, even though he's perfectly capable of doing the work. Also, if one sibling doesn't want to try at all, then other brothers and sisters might follow suit to avoid standing out or showing up the sibling.

In general, labels tend to cause more harm than good, and are best avoided. Even if parents resist putting a label on their children, sometimes the kids get stuck with one anyway. Here are some ways parents can help their children overcome "label" competition.

❑ ❑ ❑

COMPETITION SNAPSHOT

The Scenario: Your six-year-old daughter doesn't want to try anything because her older siblings—a seven-year-old brother and an eight-year-old sister—excel at everything they do. The older siblings receive numerous compliments for their "amazing" abilities, particularly in sports. Now the six-year-old wants nothing to do with physical activities. What can we do to encourage her participation?

The Solution: Stop asking her. Counterintuitive? Perhaps, but pushing her to do sports will likely not help the situation. Ask her—when her siblings are not around—what activities she'd like to try. Then see if there's a class or group in which she, and she alone, could become involved. Don't allow her siblings to attend the class or group; let her have this all to herself.

Then to lower competition in your home, don't talk so much in a family setting about how well the older sibs are doing. Ask different questions about their sports that change the focus from them to someone else, such as "Who did you think played well today?" Also make sure you're not contributing to the competitive atmosphere by praising your older children too much. This should help your younger daughter find her own special place and also help your older children realize it's not all about them and their "amazing" abilities.

❑ ❑ ❑

Kill competition with kindness. It can be hard to compete with someone who is nice to you. Therefore, one of the most straightforward ways is to create a climate of kindness.

Remember the advice of Proverbs 11:17: "A man who is kind benefits himself, but a cruel man hurts himself." Banish harsh language from your home; instead, uplift one another and praise each other's accomplishments, not excessively, but with sincerity. (See chapter 2 on how to teach kids to think the best of each other.)

As psychologist Eileen Kennedy Moore said in a *U.S News & World Report* article about sibling rivalry, "Create a climate where the siblings are encouraging each other or congratulating each other or consoling each other if things don't go well. . . . If sibling competition happens in that context, then it's just easier to handle . . . no matter which sibling wins, the family wins."[2] The Harbaugh brothers and the Williams sisters seem to embody the sentiment that to be competitive doesn't mean one has to abstain from being kind.

Practice losing and winning. The drive to win—and to be number one—is strong within us all, and it takes time for children to develop the inner fortitude to not get overly upset at losing or to become too boastful when winning. It might seem strange to think children need to rehearse how to win and lose graciously, but it's true. The safe confines of the family are a great place to learn how to be a good sport.

We've tackled this by instituting a weekly family game time. Each Sunday afternoon at four o'clock, we gather around the dining room table for a board or card game, which the children take turns picking. Besides enjoying time together, we keep an eye out for unsportsmanlike behavior both during and after the game, gently correcting improper responses to setbacks and victories. We reinforce that in order to play, we must all be willing to win or lose—and to do both without gloating, teasing, or throwing a fit. This puts competition into its proper place and aids the children in developing a correct attitude about both losing and winning.

Douse bragging. A child who always toots her own horn fans the flames of competition. Siblings probably will have little tolerance for a braggart in the family, but in case sibling pressure doesn't alleviate the problem, as a parent, you can help the child break the boasting habit by instituting the "one to three" rule. This simple rule helps the child regain control of his tendency to boast. For every one "brag" the child says about himself, he must say three equally nice "brags" about the sibling or siblings to whom he's talking. Generally, bragging feeds on a feeling of superiority, so if a child must say boastful things about himself to a sibling, it can take the fun out of it if he has to compliment the hearer—and likely put an end to his bragging ways.

Reduce child-driven labels. It's not just the parents who contribute to keeping the status quo in families with labeled kids. Often, it's the kids themselves who embrace the label—and then defend that domain from all comers. Thus, you see a brother talking a younger sister out of playing basketball for fear that her talent on the court might eclipse his. A sister might discourage her younger brother from trying out for the debate team because she doesn't want to share the spotlight with him. In those examples, the sibling feels an ownership of the label, identifying with it so strongly that he can't bear to have another sibling even attempt to play the same sport or earn the same academic achievement.

We should realize what's underneath the actions or words (jealousy), in order to assist in getting rid of the label. That jealousy is at the root of many a sibling conflict. In fact, around a third of parents (35 percent) in my informal sibling rivalry survey said that jealousy of siblings caused most of the squabbles their kids had. More times than not, a child will cling to his label because of concern a sibling may outshine him in "his" area of expertise. This jealous guarding of identity could arise from a lack of confidence in his abilities or it could simply be selfishness, not wanting the limelight to shine on someone else. Whatever the reason—and as a parent, don't waste time trying to pinpoint the why, as it's enough to recognize the jealousy— we should deal directly with the outcome.

If left unchecked, jealousy and its companion, envy, will sour the sibling relationship. As James 3:16 states, "For where jealousy and selfish ambition exist, there will be disorder and every vile practice." Point out your child's jealousy and remind him of its antidote: sincere praise and joy in another's good fortune. Saying, "Congratulations," out loud has a good effect on the heart. Talking about jealous feelings in light of the positives in the child's life puts those destructive feelings to rest. For example, if a child expresses jealousy about a sibling's good news, a parent could point out the child's own recent good fortune and how happy the sibling was for the child. Sometimes, acknowledgment of the child's envy can allow the child to put it behind him, as in, "I know you wish you could have scored a winning goal, but right now, you need to be happy for your brother."

At times, one child in the family tries to turn everything into a competition. When that happens, instruct the other children to simply respond with "you won" or "congrats" each time the child gloats over coming in first in his own imaginary game. This turns the competition over who gets on shoes first or who ate dinner faster into a boring game because the child can play only if the other siblings participate. By taking the wind out of his sails, the child should eventually stop the never-ending competitiveness over everything.

Eliminate teacher-driven labels. Adding to the child's ownership of a label identity are his teachers, especially for those brothers and sisters who attend the same school or who are in the same school district. Good teachers attempt to avoid this unconscious tendency but it's a natural response when seeing a younger sibling to assume you know something about him because of knowing his older sister. This can apply to coaches of sports, too, who sometimes view a sibling as having the same aptitude for a certain game as a sibling.

There are some ways parents can work with teachers to avoid this problem. First, list the differences between the two children. This might seem elementary, but it can be helpful to say to the teacher, "Johnny loved science, but Herbert's more into math equations." For sports, give your child permission to say no to playing the same sport as a sibling. For instance, if you have more than one boy, and the oldest boy is good at basketball, the younger ones might feel pressured to try out for the team by the coach.

We've experienced this firsthand with our four children, whose birthdays paired them back-to-back grade-wise: currently, fifth and fourth for our girls, and first and kindergarten for our boys. The older pair have "shared" teachers for first and third grades so far, and we made it a point at back-to-school nights to tell the teacher a few points of differentiation between the girls to help the teacher avoid labeling the younger as "same as older sister."

Second, have your child practice a response to comments by a teacher that equates him to an older—or younger—sibling. For example, if a teacher says, "You're Sally's little brother, so you must be good at math," the child can say politely, "I really enjoy creative writing." That type of reply alerts the teacher that the child isn't the same as the sibling and can help the teacher keep that in mind for the future. Honing some general replies also assists the child in jettisoning the mantle of expectations a teacher may have placed on him because of a sibling association.

Overall, harmful competition can spur sibling rivalry and hamper good brother and sister interactions. Remember, too, that the triggers that escalate competition can vary from family to family. In addition, parents should ensure that each of their children realize how much Mom and Dad love and care for them as individuals by telling them so on a regular basis and by spending one-on-one time with each child. (Chapter 8 will explore how parents can spend individual time with their children.) By recognizing how competition can hurt the sibling relationship and by guiding kids to have fewer harmful competitions, parents can reduce the climate for sibling rivalry in their homes.

"Comparison is a death knell
to sibling harmony."

—Elizabeth Fishel

Comparison/Favorites 4

Parents have been picking favorites from among their children since time began—to disastrous consequences. As Jeffrey Kluger pointed out in his book *The Sibling Effect*:

> It's one of the worst-kept secrets of family life that every parent has a preferred son or daughter—and the rules for acknowledging it are the same everywhere: The favored kids stay mum about their status—the better to preserve the good thing they've got going. The unfavored kids howl about it like wounded cats. And on pain of death, the parents insist that none of it is true.[1]

If you think children are unaware of parental preferences, think again. Studies have shown that favoritism is practically universal in families. For example, a University of California, Davis, study found that 70 percent of dads and 65 percent of moms had an obvious favorite among their children, typically the older sibling.[2] Sociologist Jill Suitor's research discovered that parents preferred one child over another in one-third to two-thirds of U.S. families.[3] Whether favored or unfavored, children who know which they are never forget it.

The proliferation of biblical and literary examples shows how favoritism wrecks families and sibling interactions. Favoritism rarely has any positive outcomes, and most such tales should be read as cautionary. One well-known biblical example is Jacob (later called Israel) and his son, Joseph. You would think Jacob, given how he struggled with his own father's preference for his older brother, Esau, would have tried harder to avoid playing favorites with his offspring. But Jacob ignored that lesson from his childhood and doted on Joseph. Genesis 37:3-4 doesn't leave us any doubt as to how Jacob viewed Joseph: "Now Israel loved Joseph more than any other of his sons, because he was the son of his old age. And he made him a robe of many colors. But when his brothers saw that their father loved him more than all his brothers, they hated him and could not speak peacefully to him."

The favoritism caused his brothers to feel such hatred that they couldn't even talk to Joseph nicely. Those hard feelings led Joseph's brothers to sell him into slavery. Because of his marked preference for Joseph, Jacob ended up believing his beloved son had been torn apart by wild animals. While God used those circumstances for good—Joseph becomes a savior to his people during a famine—most family instances of parental favoritism don't turn out as well. Instead, favoritism creates a sibling rivalry that often takes decades to heal—if the rift is mended at all.

Whether we like it or not, all parents have compared their children one time or another. The more we compare, the more we are likely to develop a favorite among the children. While most of us would automatically deny having a favorite, most kids would probably say their parents have a preference for one child in the family. "I worry that one of my children will connect more easily with me and that will come across as favoritism and cause a rivalry," said Cindy Damon of Fairfax, Virginia.

Sometimes, siblings work together to use that favoritism to their collective advantage. Brothers and sisters scheme to work the system to their shared benefit, such as sending in the "favored" child to ask for something from Mom or Dad. I've seen this happen in families, where the children will send in the youngest child or oldest son to ask a favor of Mom or Dad. Sometimes the parents acknowledge they can't refuse the child anything, and sometimes they will roll their eyes at the audacity of the children to "work the system."

While we might smile at the thought of kids using "favoritism" to their advantage, playing favorites can tear the sibling fabric. Long-term favoritism leads to resentment, envy, guilt, strife, and a host of other problems, which impact both individuals and the family unit as a whole. For instance, psychotherapist Jeanne Safer, who interviewed estranged adult siblings for her book *Cain's Legacy: Liberating Siblings from a Lifetime of Rage, Shame, Secrecy and Regret*, found that parental favoritism contributed to the serious contentious nature of their relationships.[4] That's a legacy we should work to avoid if at all possible.

Patterns of favoritism can become ingrained in the family unit, but the fluidity of family life may help to balance out those preferences. Favoritism can move from child to child, depending on situations in which the family operates. For example, a child could lose favored status because something she does displeases a parent, while a younger child could move into the top spot because an older child leaves home. But that doesn't mean parents can't take steps to largely avoid favoritism in general. Let's examine in detail some of the ways we can put the lid on preferences in our families.

Recognize the truth. We all compare our children sometimes. It's unavoidable to be completely unbiased toward our offspring, especially our firstborn. As Kluger put it, "No parents are quite as giddy as first-time parents, nor quite as inclined to see their child as uniquely perfect, gifted, and deserving of their emotional and material resources."[5]

That investment can lead to favoritism—often the first-born is the perceived "teacher's pet" of the parents—but if we realize our own tendency toward favoritism, we can use that knowledge to nip those inclinations in the bud. Therefore, simple awareness can make us less likely to fall into favoritism. "We tried to be consistent and not favor one child over another," said Janet Marney of Fairfax, Virginia, of her two sons. "It is especially hard if you have a special needs child. (One son had ADD, so he was more difficult to deal with in certain situations.) But you have to overcome it or it will lead to sibling rivalry."

Know your prejudices. We all have biases when it comes to family and children. Some cultures place more value on the firstborn male child, while others treasure the oldest offspring regardless of gender. Some parents show more affection to a child because of gender, either the same as themselves or the opposite. This can be manifested in scenarios as the mom who adores her son and the dad who becomes putty in the hands of his little princess.

Narcissism plays a key role in gender preferences by parents. We often favor the child who acts most like us. Sometimes, we react to those partialities by conforming or by heaping attention on the perceived "left out" child. We also can favor the child who is most different from us. Other times, it's the kid who reminds us of a favorite relative who catches our attention.

While we can't change the prejudices of others, we can modify how we react to such biases and how we interact with our children. Look at your extended family to see if there is any cultural or familial favoritism. If there is, inspect how you and your spouse react to those biases. Then take some time for introspection as to your own attitudes toward your children. Questions to ask include:

- Am I showing favoritism because of gender?
- Am I showing favoritism because of age (both older or younger)?
- Am I showing favoritism because of likeness or unlikeness?
- Am I showing favoritism because of how others treat my children?
- Am I showing favoritism to "make up" for a child's handicap or special needs?

Honestly answering those queries will put you on the path to identifying and correcting favoritism in your own heart. Being aware of your particular tendency toward preferring one child over others will put you on guard against constantly showing that favoritism.

Acknowledge the favoritism. Along with knowing our inclinations, admitting that we sometimes do for one and not the others can alleviate feelings of favoritism among our children. "I'm open about why I did this or that for one child and why the other is now receiving this from me," said Julie Arduini of Youngstown, Ohio. The child may not fully comprehend your reasons, but he will understand that you know he could perceive your actions as playing favorites. That very concession can do wonders to diffusing favoritism and its impact on siblings.

When parents couple that acknowledgment with a reminder that the child's turn for special treatment is coming, that can dispel any lingering animosity toward the "favored" sibling. "I let them know why we need to allow one child to do something the other cannot," said Michelle Boice of Manassas, Virginia. "Also, I let them know that sometimes, I do something special with one when the other isn't there and vice versa." (Chapter 8 will reflect more on how regular one-on-one time can help dismantle feelings of favoritism.)

Don't compare. This can be one of the hardest things not to do, but comparing one child with a sibling is detrimental to sibling harmony. As parents, one way we fall into the comparison game is when we comment to one child about another's behavior, good or bad. For example, Suzie breaks a glass, and we say, "Why can't you be more careful like your brother?" Or Bryon gets a hard-earned B on his science project, and we say something like, "Your sister got an A on that project when she was in fourth grade."

To the child, this type of language implies that he is not good enough or that his parents love the sibling used for comparison more. This also pressures the praised sibling to perform at a top level at all times, while simultaneously decreasing the value of the child. "We try to keep from comparing our children and to love them for who they are," said Cindy Damon of Fairfax, Virginia.

Instead, describe what you saw or what you mean only about the child in question. For instance, for the above example about the grade, you could have said, "You worked hard on that project, so you must be proud your teacher recognized that." Or for the broken glass example, you could have said, "Dry your hands better next time and the glass won't be so slippery."

For something that more than one child does, such as school, music lessons, or sports, do not compare one child's progress with a sibling. Look at tests and report cards separately, and don't let the other siblings interject comments about the child's grades while you're perusing the test or report card. Talk with each child separately about information from parent-teacher conferences and any sensitive topics, such as discipline issues, struggles with schoolwork, or trouble with teammates. Don't turn one child's problems into a sideshow attraction for the other kids. As I frequently tell my children when they ask what I discussed with a sibling, "It's none of your business." If the kids want to compare or share grades with their siblings, then let them. But we shouldn't be seen as comparing grades or anything else among our offspring.

Ditto with progress on musical instruments or on a sports team. Each child will advance at his own pace, which might be faster, slower, or similar to the pace of a sibling. We need to keep this top of mind when talking with our children about shared activities. For example, while nearly two years separate our two daughters in ages, Naomi and Leah are one year apart in school. When Leah started kindergarten (and Naomi was in first grade), her father and I adjusted our expectations and made a deliberate effort not to compare Leah's progress with Naomi's kindergarten year. Now with our two boys in the same situation of having back-to-back grades in school, we make it a point to mentally wipe the slate clean at the start of every school year for each child to avoid falling into the comparison trap. We also apply that to piano lessons and any other activity overlap. This also helps us to enjoy the progress each child makes as an accomplishment of her own, not an extension of an older sibling.

Along with that, we shut down any comparisons among our children relating to school or other activities, reminding the older ones of their own limitations when at the grade of the younger sibling. That includes not allowing an older child to interrupt while the younger one shares something from school that the older one did in the past. That practice has helped to minimize sibling conflict over comparisons and gives the younger siblings a chance to shine by themselves.

Watch your praise. Overall, praise should be used sparingly with children. Many parents believe lots of praise encourages their children and leads to high self-esteem. However, according to family psychologist John Rosemond, contrary to popular belief, praise doesn't raise self-esteem.[6] Children constantly heaped with lots of compliments, even for mediocre or failing efforts, find themselves overwhelmed by any obstacle. Kids with high self-esteem tend not to try as hard because they become afraid of failure. In addition, Rosemond notes that a child with high self-esteem constantly seeks praise for everything she does—no matter how average or poor her performance. Constant, excessive praise of one child leads to resentment among siblings.[7]

That's not to say you can't praise your child. What it does mean is that parental praise should be done with economy and care. Here are some guidelines to make praise worthy of being spoken.

- *Stick to the point.* Be as specific as possible. By using a precise reason for the compliment, parents can evade jealousy among the children that can come of too general praise. Don't say, "You did a good job." Do say, "The bathroom sink really sparkles!"

- *Avoid words like "always" or "never."* Praise should be for something in the present, not the past or future. Don't say, "You always do such nice work." Do say, "You raked the yard wonderfully today."

- *Offer praise on a regular basis, but not every day.* The more you praise, the more the child craves compliments. One way to tell if you have been offering too much positive reinforcement is to see if your children ask you lots of praise-hinting questions for ordinary things, such as, "Do you see how well I packed my book bag?" or "Look how I made my bed." Too much praise of a child makes those commendations less special.

- *Make it count.* This goes along with being specific, but with the added admonishment to ensure what's being praised is worthy. A child who receives an A on a test doesn't necessarily need heaps of praise if it's for a subject in which she excels. However, a child who struggled with fractions but misses only two questions on a test deserves recognition of her achievement. Remember that a child praised for every paper, test, completed assignment, or task will soon stop swinging for the stars in anything. A child who knows that she can overcome failure will be more likely to push herself to excel.

- *Praise one-on-one.* Make sure you provide praise separately more than in a group setting. That gives the child in question a chance to bask briefly in the glow of parental approval all on her own. If the entire group has done something you wish to compliment, by all means do so when all are present. Occasionally, a child will do something really special. Then it would be appropriate to share with others. The general rule of thumb should be that the one (or ones) worthy of the praise should be the only recipients of the commendation.

- *Praise fairly.* You don't have to keep actual score, but this is one area where you should pay attention to how often you compliment each child. If you've found yourself only complimenting one child—or praising one more than the others—reduce your overall praise quota. "I try to give compliments and praise to all of my three children," said Ashley Turner of Birmingham, Alabama, adding that it helps to lower sibling conflict when they see that all receive compliments at some point.

Recognize differences. As discussed in previous chapters, our children, while sharing some of the same characteristics and features, are in fact individuals. You simply can't lump all of your kids together. Consider what makes your child unique and yet connected to the family as a way to avoid comparison. "Grant that each child is his or her own person," said Tracie, from Sterling, Virginia. "Then listen and make sure they know they are each loved completely."

In our family, I've tried to think about what I love about each child as an individual to help me not unconsciously choose a favorite. When with a child, I try to learn more about what makes that child tick. In the process, I've found that I relate better to my children as a result—and that my frustration at their misbehavior is tempered by recalling what makes them different.

"We treat them as individuals but also as siblings," said Karen of Milford, Delaware. She personalizes little things, such as a favorite food in the child's lunchbox, but also picks activities for the entire family to enjoy together. "I'd tell them that they might not like this activity, but the next one, they may love," she said, pointing out that it halted grumbling among the siblings and improved family time.

Emphasize each one's talents. This accompanies recognizing their differences, but it takes it a bit further by incorporating what each child excels at into the family fabric. This also can give kids permission to do things differently than their siblings. "I try and think of them as individuals—they aren't the same and they don't have to try to be," said Alice of Vienna, Virginia. "I appreciate and love different things about each one."

Use the suggestions in the "Watch Your Praise" section to highlight talents. For instance, rather than saying, "Suzie's better in math than Simon," spin the focus to "Suzie's good at fractions. Simon has a knack for addition." That gives each child his area of competence without comparing or denigrating the ability of the other. Jennifer Coffin of Fairfax, Virginia, put it this way: "I see each one's gifts and shortcomings, and learn as a parent how to address both, hoping they would grow up to be humble and yet shine in the gifts the Lord gave them."

Take turns. As the next chapter will discuss in detail, parents shouldn't aspire to fairness. That's not to say being even-handed at times is bad for our children. By parceling out "turns" for some things, such as chores or picking the family flick for the weekly movie night, parents can lessen feelings of favoritism. The general rule of thumb should be that if the activity under consideration could easily fit into a rotation among the kids, then it's probably okay to have them take prescribed turns. In our family, we draw names to see the order in which the children will place the Nativity characters on our Advent calendar. This system has basically eliminated cries of favoritism, although lingering doubts as to the fairness of the system prevails some years.

Attention doesn't have to be equal. We often fall into the trap of wanting to be so precisely fair with time spent with our kids that we overlook them as individuals. Some kids may require more parental attention because of age (infants and toddlers), health (sickness or chronic disease), or special needs (academic, mental, or physical). Most families experience giving one child more attention for a period of time for a variety of reasons that could be temporary or permanent. "We try to give both of our children encouragement, love, and attention," said Elizabeth Crocker of Reston, Virginia. "However, my son simply needs more attention from us, and my daughter—the younger one—is more independent."

While even the most long-suffering sibling won't always understand that a brother or sister needs extra attention, discussing the reasons—to a limited extent—with the child can lessen resentment and hurt feelings. Just be aware that your explanations won't completely sway the children to your way of thinking. No child yet has said to a parent, "Mom, when you put it that way, I agree with you wholeheartedly that Jimmy should receive more of your attention today." In the case of a long illness or special circumstances, you would be wise to develop a plan to provide individual time with all the children, not just the one who needs more attention now.

□ □ □

COMPARISON SNAPSHOT

The Scenario: Your two kids each insist that you are favoring the other. How can you convince them you aren't playing favorites?

The Solution: You can't. What you can do is examine your own motives for the decisions you make concerning the kids. Are you thinking of them as individuals? Are you allowing your feelings of frustration about behavior to color your interactions with one or the other? Are you comparing one with another on a frequent basis? Are you holding up one sibling as the "good" example too often? Spend some time reviewing your own actions and see if you can pinpoint what might be convincing the children that you have a favorite. If, after you correct any behaviors on your part that could be contributing to their feelings, they still howl about favoritism, you can probably chalk it up to the fact that kids love drama, and ignore the comments. Eventually, as you work on keeping comparisons out of your home, they will stop talking about favoritism and realize that they're both your "favorites."

□ □ □

Cut down on negativity. Never allow a child to be labeled in any way, especially with words such as *klutz, clumsy, shorty, shrimp, fatty, dumb,* or *stupid.* The child assigned such a label, however harmless it appears to be on the surface, will come to resent that and likely look at an unlabeled sibling as receiving more parental favor. If it's a sibling who has labeled the child, that can create more stress on the relationship. (See chapter 3 for more on how to avoid labels and competition.)

Also strongly discourage a child who puts herself down because she doesn't shine in an area like her sibling. Sometimes, children not favored turn their disappointment inward instead of outward forms of aggression. It's good to remind all children that God has given each of us our own talents and abilities. He expects us to use them for his glory—not perfectly, but with our whole heart.

Along with this, do what you can to halt criticism between siblings. One sibling should not be picking another to pieces. Whenever you come across such critiquing that isn't done in love (and let's be honest, most of the time it likely won't be for the edification of the one being evaluated!), put an immediate stop to the discussion. Privately talk with the critiquer about why her comments aren't appropriate. Then talk with the one being criticized about how perfect she is in the sight of God. (See chapter 2 for more details on how to accomplish this.)

Point of view. Favoritism also can be overcome by helping our children see the other's point of view. As with competition, putting yourself in your child's shoes can help to halt comparisons. "I try to see it from each child's point of view, then explain that to the other child," explained Paula of Flower Mound, Texas.

Part of that process should be to avoid making snap judgments based on a surface glance or insufficient information. We also should hear from both children before making any decision and keeping our biases in mind as we do. "When they have conflicts, I also listen to both sides of the story rather than assume my son did something because his sister complains or whines the loudest," said Tennille Shields of Meadville, Pennsylvania.

Talk behind their backs. Don't discuss with your spouse one child in front of that child or his siblings. Make it a practice when discussing a child—either about good or bad behavior— to close the door to keep prying eyes and ears from eavesdropping. Children are nosey beings and love to hear discussions about other kids, especially siblings, but you don't want to feed that need unnecessarily. Avoid drawing the child or her sibling into the discussion when she doesn't need to be involved.

Sharing concerns or praise about a child with your spouse within the hearing of the child or her siblings can breed discontent, resentment, or feelings of worthlessness or pride in the children. Remember that your offspring do not need to be privy to everything you and your spouse talk about relating to them. Repeat, "It's none of your business," as often as needed to curb their desire to know what's happening with brothers and sisters.

Know your reactions. Have you ever caught yourself grimacing when one child does or says something? We all convey our thoughts and feelings through body language and facial expressions. What we often don't realize is that these nonverbal cues can be easily read—and misinterpreted—by our children. Sometimes, what our kids see on our faces can be just as devastating as what comes out of our mouths.

Children absorb information about their own value from the very beginning, which should cause us to modulate our tone of voice and expressions as much as possible. Even when frustrated, mothers and fathers need to remember that expressing anger, disappointment, and exasperation to a kid is okay. However, we shouldn't let our countenance or body language show scorn, ridicule, or repulsion.

To help change what we might be unaware of doing, ask your spouse to let you know if your face or body shows displeasure or favoritism when talking to one or more of your children. If one child makes us wince more than the others, then we need to work on our expressions. Having a code word for our husband or wife to say (such as "pickles" or something equally offbeat) when catching a glimpse of the wrong look can assist us in altering that habit.

Focus on one. We also need to keep our eyes on the child in front of us and not on the others in the house. Sometimes we hear what one child's saying, but our thoughts immediately jump to another. I find myself doing this when all the kids come home from school, so I've made it a practice to let one child talk to me at a time, reminding the others to wait their turn. At other times, we allow ourselves to be distracted by our phones, computers, and tablets. Thus, we end up missing what the child in front of us is saying or doing. Establishing times of electronic-free communication, such as immediately after school or at the dinner table, could help you to focus on each child in turn, and thus facilitate a better relationship between siblings as well.

We should also allow the child to bask in the glow of victory one-on-one with Mom or Dad before letting the whole world know. For instance, if a child does something well, such as a good grade on a test or winning a spot on a school team, congratulate the child but refrain from broadcasting the news to the rest of the family. Instead, let the child share his achievement with Dad, his siblings, friends, or relatives. This helps keep the attention on the child and allows the child to share his good news (or not, his choice). Now this doesn't mean at times you as a parent couldn't tell someone about your child's achievement, but make it a rule not to do so on a regular basis.

Overall, remember that explaining to your children how you don't have favorites will likely not result in alleviating concerns for the simple reason that children are not logical beings. Kids operate on an entirely different plane of reasoning than do adults. If you doubt this, listen to a child's explanation of his behavior—it often will not make any sense to your adult ears. Since our explanations tend to not jive with their perceived reality, we might as well save our breath. Instead, use the suggestions in this chapter to make sure we as parents are not inadvertently contributing to the comparison and favoritism in our homes.

"A sibling may be the keeper of one's identity, the only person with the keys to one's unfettered, more fundamental self."

—Marian Sandmaier

Separate and Unequal (Fairness)

"It's not fair!" is one of the rallying cries of childhood. At any given moment, somewhere in the world, a child is sure he's not getting a fair shake. You can't blame kids for coveting fairness. After all, the concept of fairness seems to be wired into our DNA: Scientific research has discovered that our brains react to perceived inequity the same way as when we respond to the things that disgust us.[1]

That ingrained sense of fairness makes us hypersensitive to any slight or perceived inequality. The English language reflects this with its overabundance of idiomatic expressions about fairness. A *fair shake* means treating someone fairly, while *fair and impartial* refers to being unbiased and just, generally in the legal sense. *Fair play* or *play fair* both signify no cheating in a game or competition, as does *fair and square*, which addresses being fair within the rules. *One's fair share* indicates the person should get the same as others receive. We also crave *square deals* (no cheating) and a *level playing field* (the same opportunities as everyone else). We want things to be *fifty-fifty* or *even steven* (not more or less than another). All those phrases point to an obsession with fairness.

Our children have fully internalized this and use nearly every opportunity to invoke the "fairness doctrine." These questions from our kids ring out in practically every family at some point: "Why do I always have to do this?" "Why does [sibling] get a pass and I get punished for the same thing?" "How come [sibling's] piece of cake is bigger?" Often these queries, delivered in an aggrieved tone of voice, catch parents off guard and provoke angst as Mom and Dad start worrying about whether or not they are treating their children fairly.

That our children have absorbed a desire for fairness should come as no surprise, especially when fairness is emphasized in school (as it should be among peers). After all, isn't that our own heart's reflexive cry whenever life disappoints? However, what we as adults understand is that fairness can be rather complicated. The younger the child, the less able the child is to comprehend the concept of equality at all. Children have a limited understanding of fairness in that they want things to be fair for them, without exceptions or explanations.

As they grow, kids accept that fairness has more nuances. When a child says, "It's not fair," he doesn't mean that in the true sense of the word. It's because at age six, he doesn't get to stay up as late as his ten-year-old sibling. Or at age eight, he has to do more chores than his four-year-old sister.

It's not just the kids who jump on the fair play bandwagon—we often bend over backwards to treat our children fairly. More than 86 percent of parents participating in my sibling rivalry survey said they try to treat their children fairly or equally. "I strive to be fair and consistent with my five children," said Christina Tarabochia of Tigard, Oregon, in a typical response. "Everyone has relatively the same expectations and we talk a lot if something looks unfair."

Almost as soon as parents know a second child will be joining their family, they begin to talk about being fair to both children. Nowadays, it's rare that a mother won't fret about giving each child exactly what she needs without neglecting the other children in the household. This idea of fairness also appeals to our American democratic sense. When Thomas Jefferson wrote in the Declaration of Independence the words "that all men are created equal," he was echoing the biblical idea of equality: we're all the same before God. As the apostle Paul puts it in Galatians 3:28: "There is neither Jew nor Greek, there is neither slave nor free, there is no male and female, for you are all one in Christ Jesus."

Practicing the fairness doctrine doesn't lead to generosity and gentleness of spirit but to grumbling and hoarding. Among siblings, pursuit of fairness as a parent can create conflict, frustration, and disappointment because each child will be constantly assessing everything to make sure things are distributed evenly. Even if you strive for fairness within your family, your children will still find things to pout about, as in "He got more icing on his piece of cake than I did" or "She got new shoes and I didn't."

Parents who have attempted to be absolutely fair in regard to their treatment of their children can attest that playing fair does not eliminate sibling conflict—rather it can ratchet up the rivalry to new heights. Fairness doesn't mean everyone in the family gets equal treatment, good or bad. That would put parents on the same footing as children, which isn't good for the family structure. Like effective leaders, parents should act primarily for the purpose of bringing out the best in their children. Being fair in all things to all children isn't in anyone's best interest. "Being fair is not synonymous with treating every child in an identical way,"[2] writes Melody Spier in her blog.

Central to the fairness issue is the overlooked fact that each child has a unique experience within the family unit, with twins being the only possible exception. Every child's experience in his family is largely linked to his position in that family. Basically, this means that Mom and Dad parent differently with each subsequent child. For example, they might have been more uptight with the first, more relaxed with the second, and downright flexible with the last.

Also, the child's temperament plays a crucial role in parental treatment. An easygoing toddler may need less vigilance than an active climber. These factors combine to make each child experience the family in a different way. This means that parents really can't be fair even if they wanted to treat their children equitably. This also relates to discussions in previous chapters about how parents should embrace the differences in their children and rear them according to those distinctions.

Here are some areas that most parents attempt to play fair with their children, why it's not necessary or good for the kids to do so, and ways to correct this habit.

Love

This may come as a shock, but we don't love our children exactly the same. It's an impossible task because each one is unique. However—and this is a big *however*—that doesn't mean we love any one less than another. We love each of them differently yet with the same intensity of feeling. For example, we love our mom just as dearly as our spouse, but you wouldn't say you loved your mother and spouse the same, right? It's the same with our kids: We love them each in a special way that's exactly right for them as individuals.

That means our love for them is grounded in more than just the fact that they are our children. As a result, our love for them will be stronger and more durable, more able to withstand life's ups and downs. If your kids haven't already, one day, each of them will ask you: "Who do you love the most?" When they do, your answer should reflect that you love each of them as an individual—therefore, no comparisons are possible. That's true love without measure, and when you really think about it, that's the kind of love our children need.

Equal

Fairness isn't the same as equality. You should strive to be fair-minded, but don't try too hard to ensure equality reigns in your home in all things. It's simply not possible to treat kids equally, and parents shouldn't even try. As we talked about in chapter 4 on avoiding favoritism, parents should determine the strengths and weaknesses of each child and focus on building on the strengths and overcoming the weaknesses. This will look different in each family, and that's okay. Remember that your family is an original, made up of individuals not found in any other unit.

Then focus your efforts on helping your children view circumstances through a better lens, one that shows them how their sense of fairness is skewed. Children have some "skin in the game," and therefore are not unbiased when it comes to fairness. They often want things "fair," but that means favorable to them, not to a brother or sister.

Start by acknowledging the feelings of the one who cries "It's not fair!" At times, simply saying, "I understand how you could see this as being unfair" can go a long way to diffusing a sense of inequality in the aggrieved child. However, don't feel you need to explain the situation to the child. If you think the child will listen, keep your explanation to a minimum because you don't want to open the door for arguments. Remind him of how God sees us all the same.

Favorites

Fairness also means not playing favorites. No child should be made the scapegoat, and no child should be Daddy's or

Mommy's pet. As we discussed at length in chapter 4, you don't have to interact with your kids the same way, but you should check your behavior from time to time to ensure you're not playing favorites.

Time

Do you scrupulously adhere to equal time for each child? The current mania for spending quality time with our children has led some parents to watch the clock in order to ensure each child receives the same amount of time and attention from Mom and Dad. Whether we do it for time we spend with our children ourselves ("I took Jimmy to the park for an hour on Tuesday, so I should play a game with Sharon tonight for the same amount of time") or for time our children spend on activities ("Robert is playing soccer this fall, so Erin should take gymnastics"), we can become a bit obsessed with time.

But all that clock watching does is give rise to a fixation on fairness. No one will win this game. "We talk about how fair doesn't mean equal," said Alice in Vienna, Virginia. "One child might need a special outing because he is going through a rough time, but that doesn't mean everyone gets a special time." What we should do is focus more on what each child needs at this moment—and realize that it doesn't always mean our time.

Discipline

Many parents also make the mistake of trying to discipline their kids in a fair manner. That sounds good, but in reality, it can only promote dissent among siblings. Consequences should address a child's own particular personality. Occasionally, a one-size-fits-all approach will work for all children. (For some examples, see chapter 7 on how to teach kids to resolve conflict.) More times than not, that sort of approach misses the mark. Just as each child should be considered his own person, so should that child receive tailored punishments most of the time.

If one child protests—or gets involved with—your discipline of a sibling, then it's best to give each child the same consequences. For example, you could say something like: "You know, you're right. Fair treatment means you both get the same thing. Since you're interfering with my discipline, you'll get the same consequences as your sibling."

FAIRNESS SNAPSHOT

The Scenario: Your two sons, ages eight and ten, usually get along just fine. But lately, whenever you have to discipline one, the other tells you it's not fair. Sometimes, they've been so convincing that you've not addressed the problem. You've explained and explained why they need to stay out of the disciplining of their brother, but they won't listen. What can you do?

The Solution: Step one is to stop explaining. They're not listening, and they're not going to listen or agree with your rationalization of why interfering is wrong. Step two is to realize that you've given the boys reason to think you don't mean what you say. So they have come to the conclusion that if one interferes with a punishment of the other, chances are good you'll back down.

Step three is to do something to fix the problem once and for all. The next time you're about to punish one and the other interrupts to plead his case that you're "not being fair," respond with: "You're right. I'm not. So now you both will receive the punishment since you interfered." Then follow through with punishing both of them. That will stop the interfering soon.

If a child protests a sentence because it was harsher than a sibling's—or if a child complains that a younger sibling wasn't punished at all for an infraction that meted discipline to that child earlier—recall that you don't owe him an explanation. If you must respond, you can simply agree with the child, as in, "Yes, I probably did punish you for doing the same thing when you were her age." Then walk away, leaving the child to stew in his own juices.

We sometimes get so bogged down with wanting our kids to understand and/or agree with our decisions that we find ourselves paralyzed from taking any action. Protestations related to discipline usually amount to nothing more than smoke and mirrors, an attempt to distract you from the matter at hand: delivering consequences for the child's misbehavior.

Giving and Receiving

Should you give the same amount to each child all the time? Some parents try to give equal presents at holidays and birthdays, while others give according to need. For example, an older child might receive an expensive gift, like a computer, for his birthday because he needs it for schoolwork. Another time, a younger sibling might receive a new bicycle because he outgrew his old one, but the older child has to keep his bike another year.

Trying to be fair like that can be time-consuming and can backfire by breeding competitiveness and nitpicking among the children. It also raises a whole host of questions. For example, how do you tally gift amounts—by what you paid for the gift or what the present is worth? How do you determine equity—by the number of presents or the monetary amount? This would be nigh on impossible in our house, where many gifts are homemade or purchased second-hand from yard sales, Craigslist, or eBay.

Instead, focus on fitting the gift to the child. If a huge lot of plastic dinosaurs will make my seven-year-old son happy, does it matter if the figurines are brand-new or gently used? If you don't become overly concerned with fairness and instead become concerned with pleasing the recipient, you'll find more joy and less tension in gift-giving.

For everyday things, such as clothing, shoes, and school supplies, treat each as an individual and address her needs at that moment. If Suzie doesn't need new socks, but Billy does, then Suzie doesn't get anything from the store. "Not everyone's going to get everything at the same time, like at birthdays, special treats at school, etc. Life isn't fair like that," said Janet Marney of Fairfax, Virginia. "Kids need to learn how to deal with unfairness because it's a more realistic outcome." By giving kids many chances to learn this important lesson that one doesn't always get something just because someone else did, your children will be better prepared to deal with life's inherent "unfairness."

Privileges

With children of varying ages, privileges generally are not distributed evenly. This sometimes triggers jealousy among siblings, especially younger brothers and sisters who envy older siblings their freedoms. But with more privileges come more responsibilities. "The oldest knows that more is expected of him right now as far as household chores, but that he also gets more privileges as the eldest," said Alice.

When young ones complain about an older sibling's liberties, you can gently remind them of the sibling's added duties. When an older sibling mutters about the carefree life of his younger sister, you can recall to his mind his extra rights. One thing to keep in mind is that our kids are not static—they learn and grow and advance. Therefore, the twin issues of privileges and responsibilities should be ones that are frequently revisited and revised as our children grow.

Fair Play

There is a sense in which fairness should matter to parents. Giving your kids equal opportunities should be one time when leveling the playing field makes sense. In other words, don't make provisions to send one kid to college but neglect to do so for the others. My parents handled this in a unique way: They offered to pay for one year of college or buy a used car for each child who graduated from high school. My oldest sister took the car, my two brothers never graduated from high school (although both have GEDs now), and my two other sisters and I received a year of college.

What can easily happen is that we take things too far and attempt to play fair in every single circumstance, which cheapens it for everyone. Betsey Kodat of Herndon, Virginia, spoke of the hard feelings her attempts at fairness created among her two daughters. "Whenever I spoke of one, I always spoke of the other. Whenever I gave one a gift, I always gave the other one something too. It did not turn out very well. My younger daughter said it ended up robbing her of her own specialness."

A good rule of thumb to keep things from becoming too bogged down in the search for fairness is to only consider equity in the big things, like cars and college. Most everything else, from activities and events to clothes and presents, can be parceled out at your discretion.

Future

Most of you reading this book probably have children still living at home, but it's not too early to think about what fairness will mean to your children after your death. Nowadays, you hear of more and more siblings turning on each other because of their parents' wills and other end-of-life documents. Even after you're gone, your kids will want to be treated fairly. Estate planning can be crucial to equitably distributing your earthly goods. Making plans now about how to handle this is a good idea. Here are a few things to consider.

First, you don't have to leave every child the same amount of money, but you should leave an explanation as to why you did what you did. Either write the reasons into the will itself or pen a personal letter explaining why you gave that child what you did. Keep your focus on the recipient and be as specific as possible. Don't say, "You don't need the money as much as Bob does." Do say, "You've been blessed with so much and we're proud of the way you've handled your finances."

Second, decide on the disbursement. Trusts, lump sums, or installments are popular, but conflict can happen if you put one adult child's share in a trust and give another a lump sum. Third, be up front with your adult children before you die about how your estate will be handled. You don't need to give details, but a basic outline will pave the way for fewer surprises later on, and may help to reduce hard feelings between siblings. Remember, you won't be there to smooth any ruffled feathers, so anything you can do now would benefit the entire family.

Above all, realize that children have a warped sense of fairness as it relates specifically to them. They have a stake in the outcome of everything, which skews their view of situations. What they think is fair and impartial often isn't in the true sense of the phrase. If we start trying to be fair in all that we do with and for our children, we will end up pleasing no one and paving the way for more sibling rivalry in the future.

"To the outside world, we all grow old.
But not to brothers and sisters. We know
each other as we always were. We know
each other's hearts. We share private family
jokes. We remember family feuds and
secrets, family griefs and joys.
We live outside the touch of time."

—Clara Ortega

The Blessing of Siblings

Parents often plan how many kids to have based on the number of children they think they can handle. Sometimes, that number is influenced by their own childhoods or by seeing how the children of relatives or friends behave. What parents usually fail to consider is what a healthy relationship with brothers and sisters gives a child. Hearing your children snipe at each other, or remembering fights you had with your own siblings, might make you forget the many blessings brothers and sisters can bring to your life and to the lives of your children. Whether you have one brother or sister, or five, being a sibling provides you with someone who "gets you" when the world doesn't, and with someone to share the joys and burdens of life.

Almost from the time of our birth, we share with siblings our most intimate thoughts, ideas, and dreams. Together, we explore, collaborate, conspire, and protect. We goad each other to do both good and bad things. We play together, torment each other at times, counsel each other, and comfort one another. For better or for worse, our brothers and sisters become a large part of who we are. Blogger Kellie "Red" wrote about the gift of siblings in her Patheos.com blog: "As the mother of a large family [of five kids], the culture is regularly telling me and my kids what we are missing, what we are sacrificing, because there are so many children. But we all need to look a little harder and see the very special and often intangible gifts that our children give to one another."[1]

Often those relationships outlast parents, spouses, and friends. With brothers and sisters, you share a history—the good and the bad. "My four siblings bless me in quite different ways," said Deb Elkink in Elkwater, Alberta, of her one sister and three brothers. "In adulthood, my sister and I entered into a friendship that grew slowly but steadily until, nowadays, I call her my best friend. . . . I don't have as intimate a relationship with any of my brothers, although we get along well and visit as travel allows."

If you look past the in-fighting, you'll likely see some of the secret—and not so hidden—blessings of having a brother or sister (or both!). As you watch your own children interact, note the many ways they support each other. Maybe an older sister helps her little brother tie his shoelaces, or an older boy takes his sister's hand without prompting to cross the street. These small gestures done "undercover," so to speak, show you more of their hearts than anything else. Write a few of those down and look at the list often, especially when sibling conflict heats up. It's a good way to remind yourself of the blessings of siblings.

What's Mine Is Yours

When your six-year-old son is walloping his five-year-old brother because the younger sibling had the audacity to play with "his" truck, it's hard to remember that one of the blessings of siblings is sharing. Whether it's toys, rooms, clothes, or playtime, there's nothing quite like having someone (usually) close to your age available for adventure. "Parents should see having multiple children as a great blessing because you provide a lab to learn how to share and to put others first," said Susan Alexander Yates, author of *And Then I Had Kids*. "I think the most difficult child to raise is an only child because they have no built-in, 24/7 siblings who will teach them how to argue or disagree in a healthy way."[2]

As kids age, shared memories of childhood adventures—and the not-so-fun things parents made you do—forge a bond that can be very strong. The fact is that siblings are the ones with us most of our lives. Siblings will likely outlive their parents, and their spouses came later in life. Brothers and sisters are probably the only ones who are more like life partners. That family history can link siblings together through the years. Brothers and sisters also share the load of family crisis, such as the death of a parent or illness of an elderly relative. Having that extra emotional support can make a huge difference in the quality of life for the siblings.

As believing parents, we know that raising our children in the faith and admonition of the Lord is part of our calling as Christians, as in Ephesians 6:4b: "Bring them up in the discipline and instruction of the Lord." It also can be one of the finest gifts we give our kids, as sharing faith strengthens the sibling relationship. "The best thing we share is our Christian faith," said Wade Webster of Plano, Texas. "Dad wasn't much into church, or spiritual stuff, but Mom sure was. All seven of us will be sitting at the feet of Jesus some day because of her influence, and it gives our relationships now as adults a special dimension."

Having faith doesn't mean smooth sailing in the sibling relationship. Brothers and sisters may get mad at each other and get into scrapes, but the proximity of living in the same house makes staying angry difficult. Siblings diffuse anger with peace offerings, such as by giving another a favorite toy or book. At times, the situation is resolved via roughhousing, laughter, or other forms of mock provocation that dissolves any remaining tension.

Most of the time, the best part of sharing that family history is the laughter that comes from remembering. Three of my siblings are eleven, thirteen, and fifteen years older than me. I used to be a little jealous of their closeness when, at family gatherings, they reminisced about their childhoods. Many stories involved crazy antics of one sort or another (that our parents never knew about or at least not the whole story), but it's the three of them laughing together over their younger years that sticks in my mind more than anything. Seeing the special link between them strengthens my desire to help my own kids build a solid foundation in childhood that will blossom into lasting friendship in adulthood.

In addition, living with siblings gives us a leg up in social settings. We become more in tune with the emotions of others, learn important social cues, and figure out how to interact with others, including members of the opposite sex if there are brothers and sisters in the household. Sisters initiate brothers into the feminine mystique, while brothers give girls clues about the world of boys.

Some parents I talked to revealed other ways that being a sibling was a blessing, such as recognizing family resemblance—both physical and behavioral characteristics—in your brothers and sisters. These traits provide an opportunity to evaluate the good, the bad, and the ugly that might be passed down through the generations. "It is a blessing to have healthy discussions on what traits are worth fostering and which ones need to be dealt with and changed," said Lynn K. of Seattle, Washington, who has three siblings.

Others talked about connecting with brothers or sisters over sports or other shared activities. While playing on the same sports team can create a more competitive environment, as talked about in chapter 3, it also can foster a closeness that endures long after childhood ends. "One of my brothers was a year ahead of me in school, and we played football together, with him being the kicker," said Wade. "I don't know how many hundreds of footballs I held for him as we practiced. Now I think we're the closest two siblings."

The bond between siblings can be especially bittersweet when parents become elderly and are in need of assistance. Having another to shoulder the work and decisions during what can be difficult times can make caring for older parents less of a burden. "You have a ready-made team to deal with the issues, information gathering, decision-making, and supporting each other to give the main caregiver breaks," said Kathleen Hurst of Schertz, Texas. "My brother, sister, and I are working together now like I would never have believed. We have different strengths that benefit my mom, who is eighty-six and in an assisted-living facility."

Those shared experiences learned in childhood can bloom into an even bigger blessing later on in life. "With Americans living longer than ever, increasing numbers of us will be launched into an old age in which we've outlived our friends, our parents, and even our spouses, while our children and grandchildren have scattered to distant cities. For plenty of us, the only ones left at the end of the dance will be the ones that brung us—the brothers and sisters who have been with us the longest, loved us the hardest, and by a wide margin, know us the best," concluded Kluger.[3]

The Ties That Bind

Have you ever seen your kids stick up for one another, even when the odds were against them? For example, a brother who defends his younger sister in a schoolyard tussle and the older sister who takes her baby sister under her wing in high school are showing faithfulness toward one another. Their actions sum up another frequent adjective siblings use to describe their brothers or sisters: loyal.

One biblical example of sibling loyalty is Moses, Miriam, and Aaron. Miriam demonstrated her allegiance to her brother Moses when he was just a baby in a basket by watching over him and returning him temporarily to his own mother (Exodus 2). Later, both Miriam and Aaron supported Moses during Israel's exodus from Egypt. Miriam sang victory songs after the Red Sea crossing (Exodus 15), while Aaron spoke for Moses before Pharaoh (Exodus 7) and held up Moses' hands while the Israelites battled the Amalekites (Exodus 17).

That Moses, Aaron, and Miriam had their own rocky times doesn't negate the fact that part of the blessing of siblings is their loyalty. "Your sibling always has your back," said Kim Luckabaugh of Fairfax, Virginia, who has two siblings. She continued, "While they may pick on you mercilessly at home, they're your strongest defender in public." Donna Mumma of St. Petersburg, Florida, who has four older brothers, added, "When you need something that you wouldn't dare ask anyone else for, you can ask them."

Siblings often defend their brothers and sisters from outsiders, drawing even closer in the process. Many adult siblings tell stories of how their brother or sister helped them out of a sticky situation. Jennifer Uhlarik of Brandon, Florida, who's one of five siblings, said her closest older brother protected her in elementary school from a playground bully. "My brother, who's five years older than me, talked to the boy who was bothering me. I don't know what he said, but the boy never came near me again," she said. "Later on in life, as I was a struggling single parent, that same brother had a knack for always being there when I needed a shoulder to cry on. Whether it was a bad day at work, a rough day parenting, or whatever, he would always 'miraculously' show up at just the right moment, give me a huge hug, and make sure I knew I was loved and things would be all right. That's not to say we always got along. At moments, we fought like crazy, but at some of the hardest moments of my life, he was there."

That loyalty also manifests itself later in life, when siblings often take the place of parents in the family dynamic after the death of a mother or father. As Kluger pointed out, brothers and sisters generally are with us for longer than our parents, aunts, uncles, grandparents, and sometimes friends. "Our mother passed away shortly after I found out I was pregnant with my first son," said Kimberli C. of Papillion, Nebraska. "Then our father died a few years later. Being an orphan in adulthood is hard. I used to talk to my mother every day, but now my sister has taken that spot. We have taken the precious traits our parents gave us and used them to give each other support or kick one another in the pants if needed."

An Understanding View

Siblings also provide a way for us to view the world from someone else's perspective. They have a knack for taking us down a peg when our egos get too inflated, and also propping us back up when life knocks us down. The trials and tribulations one sibling faces often spur the others to develop a more understanding and compassionate view of the world. "My sister's special needs influenced me to become a teacher," said Kathleen. "I spent a lot of time helping her understand information that she couldn't process easily. Very often, siblings of a special-needs kid become nurses, doctors, and teachers because of their early childhood experience assisting their sibling."

As parents, we can assist our children in interpreting the motives behind the actions. Kids rarely see the positive in a brother's or sister's deeds and often miss the fact that the sibling does care about them. As we talked about in chapter 2 on thinking the best of a sibling, we should point out the affection and admiration that a child has for her siblings, because it's not always obvious to others. Remind your kids that having a brother or sister is a blessing because he or she brings the potential of having a best friend under the same roof.

In addition, having an opposite-sex sibling gives children a different set of skills, especially when relating to a spouse or child. Brothers learn how girls talk and process information, while sisters figure out what makes boys tick. "I had understanding about raising sons from watching my brother grow up," added Kathleen. "I was ready for some things that my husband wasn't because my son's personality is like my brother's. Remembering how my brother grew out of that stage helped keep me sane while my son went through the same thing."

Relating to the same-sex sibling provides a deeper level of understanding and trust. The bonds between brothers create a strong relationship not easily broken, and the ties between sisters join them together throughout their lives. With siblings of the same gender "you have instant bridesmaids or groomsmen," said Melanie Osborne of Ashburn, Virginia, who has three brothers and three sisters. "As sisters, we talked a lot about dating, and about what clothes, colors, hairstyles, nail polish, etc., we should wear. It really brought us closer together to share those things."

A Blessing in Disguise

As you raise your children, the attachment they form will likely transcend any current conflicts and mold them into better human beings in the process. Proverbs 27:17 (NIV), "As iron sharpens iron, so one person sharpens another," could have been written for siblings. Brothers and sisters smooth our rough edges and strengthen our weak areas. "The best thing we did to help our kids see the blessing of their own siblings was to homeschool them while we lived at the end of a long gravel road in some isolation," said Deb. "Homeschooling forced me to help them learn to negotiate sibling difficulties throughout their early childhood through to their entry into high school, when they boarded away from home. They bonded together in a sure and deep friendship, and now at ages thirty, thirty-three, and thirty-five, they are still very close."

If we take the time to look at our children's interactions, we're likely to see the early stages of lasting connections. "We have always told them that God made them brothers," said Karen of Milford, Delaware, of her two boys. "They know what God expects from them and that, as their parents, we are to make sure they live that out. God gives them grace each day—and they are to give that to each other as well."

Last summer, a trip to our community swimming pool brought the blessing of siblings home to my four kids. Micah, the oldest boy and third-born, trembled on the edge of the diving board, fear fighting against his desire to jump off into the water. As his seven-year-old frame wavered, Naomi and Leah, his two older sisters, and Silas, his younger brother, shouted encouragement from the side.

Even while the minutes ticked away and Micah stayed frozen on the board, his siblings cheered him on, showering him with all the love and encouragement they had in their hearts. It didn't really matter that earlier in the day Micah had vexed his sisters because of something he said. It didn't really matter that Micah had taken one of Silas's toys that morning. All that mattered was that Micah needed them, and they were there for him, for as long as it took him to finally take that final step—and plunge into the water, his triumph celebrated by their cheers of goodwill.

"Our brothers and sisters are there with us from the dawn of our personal stories to the inevitable dusk."

—Susan Scarf Merrell

Conflict Resolution

7

Have you ever looked at your kids fighting and seen an opportunity for personal growth? Most parents don't view tussles between their offspring as anything but disruptive and damaging to the family. However, teaching our children the proper and biblical way to handle conflict can restore peace to our homes and set our kids on the path to relationship success. "I think children have to experience conflict in order to learn to resolve it," said Alice of Vienna, Virginia. "If we try to smooth it over and artificially make them act like they are all getting along and everything is fine, they never learn to deal with real problems."

The temptation for parents is to skip the teaching part and simply move to making peace themselves, but that harms children by focusing on the why of the conflict and by taking the problem-solving part of the conflict away from the children. What parents all too easily forget is that children, because of their nature, disposition, and age, are not civilized beings. That's something that needs to be taught to a child, such as when we teach them to say "please" and "thank you." Their uncivilized nature becomes apparent when a parent asks a child why he hit his sister or what outcome did he expect when he took his brother's toy. The child more times than not shrugs and shakes his head in bewilderment. He truly doesn't know the reason for his actions because he doesn't reflect that much on why he does things. That kind of thinking develops more as the child grows up. However, not knowing the *why* behind his actions doesn't mean the child lacks the ability to resolve the conflict in a more beneficial way for all involved.

Some believe that children must be genetically disposed to fighting—after all, they do it so well!—but fail to realize that kids are equally equipped to make peace. That the ability to make up is essential to their emotional and mental development is often overlooked by parents. We can't continually broker treaties between our children because then they don't learn to do it for themselves and our negotiated cease-fires don't last as long. Peace made by non-invested parties, that is, parents, never sticks as well as harmony brought about by the warring parties.

Thus, when parents get too involved in their children's disputes, they rob the kids of a valuable learning experience. Yet it's hard to resist that involvement. When their offspring fight, more than half of parents (52 percent) who took my sibling survey usually attempted to negotiate a peace between them. Thirty-eight percent generally encouraged the children to solve the problem on their own, with 8 percent typically ignoring the fighting and 2 percent taking sides or assigning blame. "I wish I had earlier on in their childhood figured out how to identify for them what the issues might be as they arose—and taught them to identify what was really bothering them beneath the fighting, so they could have dealt with the base problem," said Deb Elkink of Elkwater, Alberta. "But more often, the noise and emotional (or physical) upset demanded some sort of initial parental intervention."

As Deb pointed out, parents do have a role to play in sibling conflict because parents shouldn't leave the entire process to the children. Teaching kids how to peacefully resolve conflict is as important as letting them figure out the nitty-gritty details themselves. Ninety-three percent of my survey respondents said they consciously teach their children how to resolve conflict. As Kathleen Hurst of Schertz, Texas, put it, "We gave our kids the phrases or strategies to help them know what to do in fights—and that definitely helped keep the peace in our home."

My husband and I decided early on that we would not play referee in our children's disagreements. It was not our job to intervene when the wailing started out of sight. We would not judge who was right and who was wrong. No assigning roles of victim or villain for us. If we happened to actually see the wrongdoing, that was another thing. But we would not participate after the fact in their misunderstandings. We would give kisses but would not encourage tattling.

This chapter will provide nuts-and-bolts instruction for teaching your children conflict resolution and suggestions for how parents can stay out of the process as much as possible. Above all, keep in mind Psalm 133:1—"Behold, how good and pleasant it is when brothers dwell in unity!"—to help get you over some of the inevitable bumps along the way. The way to having your kids resolve their own conflicts won't be smooth, but the end result of little parental intervention and a more peaceful home will be worth the effort.

Scriptural Basis

The best place to start for Christian parents is what Scripture teaches about conflict resolution. Not surprisingly, the Bible has a lot to say about how to handle conflict. Parents would do well to follow the sound advice found in the Word of God and use it to lay a firm foundation upon which to build a good toolbox for conflict resolution. "Teach them what God's Word says about conflict, pray with them, have them practice, and be an example to them," said Lelia Jones of Columbia, South Carolina. "When we mess up and handle things the wrong way, ask forgiveness! We can't resolve recurring conflict without prayer and trust in the Holy Spirit to change our hearts. Pray with the child and ask for them to pray for us when we mess up."

While there are numerous passages that address conflict resolution, we'll focus on three found in the gospel of Matthew: 7:1-5, 18:15-16, and 7:12. These three sections drill down to the heart of conflict and its resolution by concentrating on our own sin, the right way to settle disagreements, and how to avoid future clashes.

Matthew 7:1-5 addresses our sinful tendency to focus on the sin of others rather than ourselves:

Judge not, that you be not judged. For with the judgment you pronounce you will be judged, and with the measure you use it will be measured to you. Why do you see the speck that is in your brother's eye, but do not notice the log that is in your own eye? Or how can you say to your brother, "Let me take the speck out of your eye," when there is the log in your own eye? You hypocrite, first take the log out of your own eye, and then you will see clearly to take the speck out of your brother's eye.

For conflict resolution to work, one needs to acknowledge one's own part in the fracas. Until that happens, there can be no true reconciliation. "We encourage them to name the sin and ask for forgiveness," said Colleen Scott of Marysville, Ohio. "Children learn to resolve conflict by turning to the Word and seeing what the Lord has to say." The *Brother Offended Checklist* is a great tool for young kids to learn how to handle offenses from both sides—offendee and offender. This resource (a laminated one-page poster and a booklet that explains the poster in-depth) uses Scripture verses to show kids what the underlying heart issue is behind typical encounters that led to conflict.

Teaching what this means to our kids helps them check their motives. While we as parents shouldn't always pursue the reasons behind our children's scuffles, kids do need to become more self-aware about the source of their actions. "I usually ask the question, 'Are you telling me to get your brother into trouble or are you telling me out of concern for your brother's well-being?'" said Alice of Vienna, Virginia. "If it's the first one, I encourage them to talk directly to each other instead of to me."

Matthew 18:15-16 shows why going outside the source of the conflict, that is, to a parent, shouldn't be the first resort:

> If your brother sins against you, go and tell him his fault, between you and him alone. If he listens to you, you have gained your brother. But if he does not listen, take one or two others along with you, that every charge may be established by the evidence of two or three witnesses.

While the brother here in these verses does refer to brothers in the Lord, the meaning of the passage is applicable to our children as well. "If one comes to me to complain about the other, I usually tell them to go to the source," said Mary of Owego, New York.

As mentioned in chapter 2, the Golden Rule as found in Matthew 7:12—"So whatever you wish that others would do to you, do also to them, for this is the Law and the Prophets"—has many applications for conflict resolution. (We will unpack this idea a bit more later in this chapter.) "We ask our children if they would want someone to treat them the same way," said Tiffany Amber Stockton of Colorado Springs, Colorado.

"I really incorporated the Golden Rule in my parenting efforts," added Carol Ozier of Decatur, Alabama. "I frequently asked them, 'How would that make you feel? How would you want someone to treat you?' and communicated about what was going on. I encourage them to learn to walk the walk, not just talk the talk, when it comes to relating to others, forgiving others, and respecting others. The Golden Rule really helped me teach many basic manners, respect for others, being responsible for your own actions, and not always putting self first."

Many parents have found it helpful to incorporate Scripture as an integral part of conflict resolution because it gives such solutions proper context, namely that conflict resolution is important because it's important to God. "I encourage them to first pray and then to humble themselves. In fights, all involved are responsible," explained Michelle Boice of Manassas, Virginia. "After prayer, they need to calm down and be prepared to listen as well as talk. They need to be ready to forgive as well as ask for forgiveness. Finally, I suggest to them to tell why they were hurt by what happened. If they still can't forgive, they are to come to us."

Now that the scriptural foundation for resolving arguments has been laid out, we'll move on to the more practical aspect. Conflict resolution has several parts, including the need for self-control, the desire for peace, the example of parents, the avoidance of violence, the requirement for kind words and calm spirits, the tools for argument, the rules for confrontation, the way to apologize, the need for forgiveness, the knowledge of involvement, the consequences of actions, and the necessity of moving past the conflict.

Self-Control

The benefits of self-discipline, while timeless in nature, have fallen out of favor in today's ultra-busy, ultra-competitive environment. In addition, the expectation of instant gratification has pushed the virtue of self-control to the back burner. Discipline of self isn't on display in the public's eye as it once was. Television reality programs show people behaving badly with little self-control of their emotions, actions, or words. At sporting events, athletes throw loud and obnoxious temper tantrums when a call or game doesn't go their way. In fact, the worse the reality TV stars and sports figures act, the better for ratings.

Maintaining self-control is an important component of conflict resolution. Exercising self-control in the midst of extreme provocation is essential to resolving conflict in a way that's fruitful for all parties involved. It's no mistake that self-control, or the more old-fashioned word *longsuffering*, is included in the fruit of the Spirit: "But the fruit of the Spirit is love, joy, peace, patience, kindness, goodness, faithfulness, gentleness, self-control; against such things there is no law" (Galatians 5:22-23).

We must remind our kids that they are masters of themselves. It seems obvious, but children do need to be told that they can control their reactions to events, people, circumstances, etc. They are not a leaf to be blown about in the wind— they have the ability to exercise control. It does take practice and perseverance to strengthen our self-control muscle. Here are some ways parents can guide their children's development of self-control.

Show your struggles. It can be difficult to teach self-mastery to our children if we don't embody it ourselves. All of us stumble in the area of self-control at one time or another. Share some of your "down" moments with your kids. For example, you could talk at dinner about how you lost your temper at work. Tell how you apologized and what steps you're taking to avoid future blowups, such as not scheduling meetings right before lunch because being hungry makes you irritable. Ask for prayer as you work through this loss of self-control. Revisit the issue later to show what progress you've made or what relapses you've suffered, and how you're continuing to press forward.

Letting them see a snippet of how you wrestle with self-mastery can encourage them in their own struggles.

Practice it. Working on self-control is no different from practicing a sport. Professional athletes, for example, often do the same drills over and over again. Self-control can be acquired by practicing it again and again. Stress that losing self-control doesn't mean the child has failed. Setbacks are inevitable. What matters most is pressing forward to try again.

Give them strategies. When kids lose self-control, it's often manifested with hitting, kicking, and screaming. Good ways to stretch that self-control muscle include:

- Counting to ten before responding
- Removing yourself to settle down away from others
- Putting your head down on a desk, if at school
- Jumping on a mini-trampoline
- Running around the outside of the house
- Having an adult say a catchphrase when things heat up

"We had our kids sit on the steps until they got themselves under control," said Christina Tarabochia of Tigard, Oregon. In our family, there have been times when a child has needed a secret word like "puppy" that we'll say when that child begins to lose her cool. That has helped the child regain control and has headed off potential quarrels with siblings.

Delay gratification. Self-discipline can be taught by not giving in immediately to a child's request. Don't let them have their way just to gain quietness. Some ways to help children learn to wait include:

- Visiting stores without buying anything for the children
- Limiting the number of presents at holidays and birthdays
- Not giving snacks before dinner
- Making them wait their turn

These types of things will help the child's self-control muscle grow.

Use rewards sparingly. Self-control is more about a child's inner life than about her outer conformance. We want the child's heart to be engaged in the waiting too. Don't give constant positive reinforcement for every compliance or good job of waiting. For example, a child should wait her turn because it's the right thing to do, not because she'll get a lollipop if she does. Otherwise, a child won't be able to wait without the promise—and deliverance—of a reward. However, every once in a while, a small reward for exceptional waiting behavior is okay.

Desire for Peace

The desire for a peaceful, calm house isn't wrong, but many times, parents try to achieve it at all costs. Intervening to have peace can be detrimental to children learning how to resolve conflict on their own—and to develop a desire for peace themselves. "We can teach our children conflict resolution by having a desire for peace, which is something you can teach them," said Susan of Waupun, Wisconsin. There are two simple ways parents can help their kids achieve peace.

Keep your distance. We parents need to let our kids muddle through most conflict resolutions on their own so that they will learn how. "We don't intervene in every dispute or disagreement, no matter how tempting it is for a parent to settle the argument in order to maintain peace," said Tiffany. Yes, we should guide them in what that looks like in the beginning, but all too often we jump in because we want the noise to stop or the chaos to abate now, not in twenty minutes. Our impatience with the often-messy way kids go about conflict resolution propels us to fix the situation for short-term peace, but that often comes at the expense of a more permanent negotiation between the warring factions.

CONFLICT SNAPSHOT

The Scenario: Your preteen daughter and young teenage son get into the name-calling like no one's business. Idiot, stupid, you've heard them all. The name-calling generally degenerates into a fight. How can we conquer this?

The Solution: You can't. Only the two of them can get a handle on this rivalry. One way to help them figure out how to stop fighting so much is to designate a small space in your home, such as a powder room, laundry room, or large closet, as the "conference" room. When the arguing commences, direct them to take it to the conference room for half an hour (set a timer). When the timer dings, ask them if they've solved the problem. Most of the time, they probably have. If not, then send them back in for another half hour.

This approach allows you to keep calm and them to discover that they can solve their own problems and will likely fight less, given they probably don't want to spend thirty minutes in a small space with their sibling every time they argue.

Bite your tongue. We have a tendency to talk too much to our kids during conflict, so staying silent while the kids hash it out is very important to establishing peace. For most fights, don't offer words of wisdom or chastisement during or after the conflict. Peace achieved by outside means never lasts as long as peace negotiated in the trenches. Above all, keep Isaiah 26:3 uppermost in your mind: "You keep him in perfect peace whose mind is stayed on you, because he trusts in you." This verse reminds us of the source of true peace—our heavenly Father—and how we would be wise to heed his directives.

Parents' Example

Parents have a lot of influence when it comes to their children's behavior. How we resolve conflict—or don't settle the disagreement—impacts how our offspring deal with discord. Do you yell, scream, pout, cry, huff, or puff? Do you clam up or say mean things? Do you let anger and disappointment simmer before blowing your top? Or do you respectfully discuss a problem with your spouse, listen to the other side, and come to a mutually beneficial compromise? How we model problem solving can have a huge impact on how our children perceive and resolve conflict. "Parents have to show the kids firsthand what it means to be respectful of others," said Elizabeth Crocker of Reston, Virginia.

But there is a right way and a wrong way to model disagreements. Here are a few ground rules to follow when showing conflict resolution in front of your kids.

Pick appropriate topics. Not every marital disagreement is fit for tender ears, as some subjects should be discussed in private. Topics that require long discussions should probably be done away from the kids, as they might tune out and miss the conversational thread and conclusion. Subjects about other family members shouldn't be talked about in public, either. A good rule of thumb is to never fight about something in front of the kids that you wouldn't want repeated to your neighbors. (Kids are notoriously bad at keeping juicy bits of family data to themselves.) Consider, too, the age of your children. A kindergartner probably wouldn't benefit from hearing a financial disagreement, but a teen might.

Don't stop halfway. Conflict resolution has a natural beginning (the source of the matter), a middle (both sides express their points), and end (both parties agree on a solution). If you only show the end without the preceding parts, kids might miss those crucial elements. Likewise, if only the middle or beginning is on display, then how to get to the final resolution could elude them. "My husband and I resolve our conflicts (rare, to be honest) in front of the children all the way to resolution," said Sharon Cartwright of Fairfax, Virginia.

Fight openly—sometimes. It shouldn't overly upset kids to see their parents in conflict every once in a while, especially if they also see how they compromise and work together to a solution in a positive way. If you keep every disagreement hidden, then your kids could develop a wrong view of marriage and conflict resolution. But that doesn't mean they need a front-row seat to every fight between their parents. My husband and I at times will either leave the room or send the kids to another room before continuing our discussion.

"I think children absorb the atmosphere of the home in more ways than one. Parents should model conflict resolution, not simply keep all their differences hidden, or children will think harmony should be automatic instead of an achievement," said Betsey Kodat of Herndon, Virginia. "We should let appropriate parts of our conflicts as parents show to let our children see how we resolve differences by understanding and compromising or agreeing to disagree. It is a process children have to learn. Seeing resolution is the most important part of this process."

Talk about the conflict. Occasionally, having a discussion with your kids about a particular conflict that has been resolved between husband and wife can be instructional to your children. For example, sometimes if a child is struggling with apologizing, I'll point out how her father said he was sorry to me for a particular thing that happened earlier that week. Reminding our offspring of our own conflict resolution can help them learn how to find solutions to their own fights.

"We tried to model positive conflict resolution. It was more like a guided exercise. We would ask our kids, 'Did you tell them what was bothering you?'" said Janet Marney of Fairfax, Virginia. "We modified our approach to their age. We were hands-on when they were little, and gradually more hands-off as they got older and took on more responsibility for themselves in every way."

Words, Not Fists

In children, especially the younger ones, frustration often erupts into striking out at the source. When that's a sibling, tears or retaliation usually follows. It's a rare family that doesn't occasionally encounter some hitting, shoving, pinching, slapping, or biting among the children.

One of the most important tools in conflict resolution is learning how to use words and not physical force to get the upper hand in a situation. "We really encourage the use of words to explain feelings, and not temper tantrums," said Charles Gluck of Herndon, Virginia. Here's how you can help your children overcome their own tendency to smack a sibling during squabbles.

Remind. How many times have you been stopped from expressing your anger by a judiciously spoken word? It seems simple, but a verbal, "No hitting," acts like a body check on a child. For toddlers and preschoolers, grab their hands as you say the words to reinforce the instruction. For older children, physically stepping between the potential combatants can redirect their thoughts.

Respect. Regard for others is hard to maintain if you call someone derogatory names. Ban name-calling and other disparaging words in your home. Sure, you won't eliminate the usage entirely, but by limiting exposure to put-downs, you build respect. Suggest alternatives for expressing feelings, such as substituting a descriptive phrase of the child's feelings for a bad name. For instance, instead of saying "You dummy," the child could say instead, "I felt sad when you wouldn't play with me." Providing concrete examples of what to say instead of bad-mouthing the sibling will give the child positive choices for future fights. "We try to equip them to work out their own conflicts with respectful words," added Sharon.

Listen. Listening is one of the hardest skills to learn at any age, and listening to another person when you're upset is difficult. Yet this is a vital tool for conflict resolution—without the ability to listen to the other party, a child misses essential clues as to the conflict's origin and solution. Listening should involve three components: the actual words, the meaning, and the proper reaction. (We'll delve deeper into this later in the chapter when we discuss the tools of conflict resolution.) "Learn to listen because most disputes are misunderstandings, so asking why the other person is upset helps clear things up in most cases," said Ruth Reid of Dade City, Florida.

Ask. Questions—from parents and siblings—uncover solutions previously not considered. Learn what kinds of questions can facilitate resolving conflicts. "My husband is especially good about asking questions that help them figure out how to solve the problem, such as, 'What can you do that will make it where both of you can have fun in this activity?'" said Cathy Martin of Ashland, Nebraska. Other questions could include, "Why are you sad?" and "What can I do to make this right?"

Encourage. Kids want to give up too quickly on anything that takes more than a nanosecond to complete, and conflict resolution is no exception. Persuade them to stick with it and to follow the resolution through to the end. "We encouraged them to tell the other how they felt as a result of the argument or fight," said Carolyn Greene of Powhatan, Virginia. "Then they had to come up with alternative behaviors for similar conflicts in the future."

Equip. Later on in this chapter, we'll tackle specific tools and rules for conflict resolution, but for now remember that teaching these to your children will prepare them to better handle future fights. "I give them the tools, such as asking the person to stop and letting them know the other's behavior hurts them," said Lelia. "I try to help them discern what is really important and what can be ignored. Above all, we stressed using kind words instead of hitting and kicking, and asked them how they would want someone to treat them."

Revisit. After the fight is over, sometimes it's helpful to go back to the scenario with your children to see what went right and what didn't work. "When they were cooled down after emotions had abated, I would bring up the issue and ask for feedback and possible ways they could have approached it," said Deb.

Just as you sometimes fail to mind your language carefully in the midst of a conflict, so will your children—or they will forgo words altogether and pummel a sibling. But by implementing these strategies into the fabric of your family, you'll help your kids use their words, not their fists, more often. "I show them how to love one another and have the wisdom to know their options and to be able to wisely choose a response," said Betsy DeMarco of Fairfax, Virginia. "We practice overlooking a minor offense, and learning to talk about it on your own or take it to a parent."

Cool Down

In the heat of battle, tempers flare, words fly, and feelings spill over into one huge mess. Many times, the initial step toward successful conflict resolution is time to calm down. (See "Controlling Anger Starts Early" on page 130 for more on how anger can be abated.) There are no right or wrong ways to accomplish this, as it depends on your children's ages and temperaments, along with the size of your home. Here is some advice from other parents on how cooling off worked for their families.

For the McGinnis family of Mount Orab, Ohio, when sibling conflict arose, Penny McGinnis made her five children sit together on the couch until they could find a resolution. Dorothy Bond-Dittmer of Akron, Ohio, preferred splitting up her children to attain calmness. "If there is a problem, we separated them until they're ready to say 'I'm sorry' to the other, no matter whose fault it is," she said.

When sibling conflict commenced, Cheri S. of Battle Creek, Michigan, banished her children together to a place far removed from earshot. "I have them go somewhere alone, like in the playroom for instance, where we can't hear them. They are quite capable of resolving the issue without our interference. Talking to them individually when they aren't fighting also helps," she said.

In our household, we'll recommend that the angry combatants go outside or to their rooms for a cooling-off period. No matter how you handle this, fostering a time for letting emotions abate can be a good move toward ending hostilities among your kids.

□ □ □

THE POWER OF FORGIVENESS

The role of forgiveness is sometimes overlooked when talking about conflict resolution. Often, not forgiving ends up hurting the person more than the fight. As discussed in this chapter, forgiveness doesn't mean not acknowledging the consequences of our actions. The apologizer should make appropriate restitution or receive proper punishment.

Our children need to know the detrimental effect not forgiving can have on their own hearts and their relationship with their siblings. The longer we hold onto our unforgiveness, the harder it will be to forgive. There are several points to make about forgiveness and its role in restoring relationships.

First, forgiveness is commanded by God. Colossians 3:12-13 tells us to "Put on then, as God's chosen ones, holy and beloved, compassionate hearts, kindness, humility, meekness, and patience, bearing with one another and, if one has a complaint against another, forgiving each other; as the Lord has forgiven you, so you also must forgive." We have no right to hold on to unforgiveness, no matter how righteous our feelings are to us.

Second, we don't forgive by our own might, but through faith in God. As the apostle Paul says in Philippians 1:6, God is working through us and will help us to forgive: "And I am sure of this, that he who began a good work in you will bring it to completion at the day of Jesus Christ." Having our children pray for the ability to forgive is vital to their learning to fully forgive.

Third, forgiveness is necessary. Jesus talked about the need to forgive in this exchange with Peter found in Matthew 18:21-22: "Then Peter came up and said to him, 'Lord, how often will my brother sin against me, and I forgive him? As many as seven times?' Jesus said to him, 'I do not say to you seven times, but seventy-seven times.'" If Jesus commands us to forgive again and again, we must be willing to do so with our whole hearts.

Fourth, forgiveness is essential to our Christian walk. Jesus doesn't beat around the bush when he says after the Lord's Prayer that our forgiveness of earthly wrongs is tied to our heavenly Father's forgiveness of our sins: "For if you forgive others their trespasses, your heavenly Father will also forgive you, but if you do not forgive others their trespasses, neither will your Father forgive your trespasses" (Matthew 6:14-15). We can't ignore this command, and we must teach our children the impact that forgiveness makes on their relationship with God and family.

Use these verses as a starting place to talk with your children about forgiveness. Make it a point to revisit this topic to instill in your children the importance of forgiveness in their lives and its role in conflict resolution.

❑ ❑ ❑

Tools for Argument

Arguments can be constructive but more times than not, the way we disagree negates any positive outcome. If your house is anything like mine, your children get into some pretty heated arguments over some pretty silly—at least to our grown-up sensibilities—things. Providing our kids with the skills to have discussions that are respectful and fruitful is one key to reducing sibling conflict. If each one has her say and feels the others listen and "get" her side, the outcome—no matter if it's for or against—usually makes everyone happy—or at least able to move on from the disagreement.

Here are some ground rules for arguments. Go over these points when all the kids are calm, then step in to guide the discussion for the first few fights afterward. But remember that your role is transitional, and thus you should ease back as soon as possible. "We've given them the tools, talked it out, walked it out, and now that they're older, we watch them take those tools and use them," said Julie Arduini of Youngstown, Ohio. "Now they rarely need my refereeing."

Blame. Who started it doesn't matter—it's how it ends that's more important, so don't get into the blame game. The truth of the matter is that all parties contributed something to the mess, maybe not right this moment, but in actions or words beforehand. Don't play detective. Instead, keep the kids focused on the issue or problem, not on whether one triggered the fight.

Calm. As stated earlier, put any resolution process on hold until all the kids are able to talk without yelling. Have them practice counting to ten before speaking, taking a deep breath, or other calming techniques to keep things civil.

Words. Enforce the no-name-calling rule and reiterate that all speech should be respectful to the other person. Each party should have a turn speaking without interruption. "Act like civilized people. Treat loved ones and family better than anyone else in the world," said Ashley Turner of Birmingham, Alabama.

Listen. Practice good listening skills in order to be fully engaged in the discussion. Active listening involves more than eye contact. Take the time to go over the active listening stages.

1. The listener needs to pay attention to the speaker. Look at her directly.
2. The listener needs to show he's listening. Use body language, such as nodding and smiling.
3. The listener needs to provide feedback.
4. The listener needs to hold off judgment. No interruptions or arguments until the speaker is finished talking.
5. The listener needs to respond by following the Golden Rule. An apology or other forms of restitution might be necessary.

Parrot. Have each child paraphrase what the other said to ensure listening skills are being used. Go over why this is important and how the speaker should gently correct the listener if her message got garbled.

Solve. Let the children suggest the solution to the problem. Resist the temptation to offer your own suggestions, especially when the kids start whining that "we can't think of how to solve this" after a minute's contemplation. During the training period, step back and tell them to let you know when they've solved the problem to everyone's satisfaction. If everyone does not agree, then it's back to the drawing board. When you think they've caught on enough to be unsupervised, let them hash it out on their own. "We worked with them to give them the skills to resolve on their own," said Elizabeth Crocker. "I was so proud when my son told my daughter she needed to share a stuffed animal and they decided to take turns on their own."

Apologize. Not every conflict needs an apology, but it's often part of the solution. We'll discuss the details a bit further on in this chapter.

Practice. Once the solution has been agreed upon, the kids should put it into practice. Any problems with the resolution that become apparent during implementation should be addressed the same way. "Children learn to resolve conflict through practice," said Mary. "The only way to learn is to practice conflict resolution. I think that as a parent, it's important to guide the process, but also to let them hash things out themselves, especially with minor conflicts."

Guide your kids through this scenario a few times with their real-world problems and revisit the steps periodically to ensure they are remembering to treat one another with respect and honor. "Walk them through it when they are with you," said Jennifer Coffin of Fairfax, Virginia. "This changes from little kids to older kids. The way we speak to them has to be age appropriate. But sin never leaves us for long. Each day we face what God has given us to do and for us as parents to teach how to love, not brag, be kind, appreciate differences, and be a servant with gifts."

Rules for Confrontation

Here are some additional thoughts on confrontation rules. Help your children see that even during an argument, rules need to be followed to ensure a better outcome.

Acknowledge the hurt. Parents must walk a fine line between being sympathetic but not being overly empathetic. We don't want to risk putting one child into a "victim" slot or "perpetrator" category by how we respond to their distress. Whenever one of my children has tears because of sibling conflict, I kiss or hug the child, usually saying something noncommittal about the distress without specifically commenting on the situation.

Children, too, need to be reminded of how to respond to the tears or hurt feelings of a sibling. "I've told my older daughter not to use her age advantage to deliberately annoy her sister just because she's older and 'wise' enough to know how to do something. And I've told my younger daughter that she cannot get upset over every single thing there is to be upset about," said Elizabeth Spencer of Battle Creek, Michigan.

Reinforce the negative impact of yelling, hitting, or retaliating in kind. Uphold the Golden Rule and Jesus' own life as examples as to how a child should respond to hurt feelings. As Jesus said in Matthew 5:39, "But I say to you, Do not resist the one who is evil. But if anyone slaps you on the right cheek, turn to him the other also." Discuss how that verse plays into real-life confrontations.

Stress compromise. In most situations, it's appropriate that the kids come up with their own solution that gives and takes from each of them. When both children give some and both "win" something, they will feel like winners. Sometimes, though, a child clearly is the one who needs to apologize or make restitution, so guiding him through that process initially can be good, although for future conflicts, you'll need to step away.

Let the solution stand. What the kids decide might seem unworkable to you, but resist the urge to tweak it. The children can work out any further details later on their own. "Remind them to 'live in the solution,'" said Kerry of Webster, Massachusetts. They will learn how to craft better solutions as they work through ones that aren't so good.

Role play. For young kids and older children, practice conflict resolution with some common situations from your home.

Go over the tools for arguments and other ideas in this chapter, but be careful not to overwhelm the children with too many details. Pick one or two things you see them doing frequently, such as name-calling or yelling, and work on those first. Then add to the mix other target behaviors that happen during conflicts when you see progress with the first ones.

Use questions. Sometimes, having a list of questions the child can ask herself during a fight can be helpful in directing the discussion in the proper direction. Carolyn Greene of Powhatan, Virginia, has three rules for confrontation:

- Is what you're saying helpful?
- Is it necessary?
- Is it kind?

Other questions include:

- What do you hope to accomplish?
- What is your goal?
- How could everyone's needs be met?

The goal of the queries is to get the children to think beyond the moment to their motives and to a solution to the squabble.

Have a "blessings jar." Sometimes, in the midst of fighting, children (and adults!) forget what they like about each other. Designate a jar or box that members can write down what they like or admire about someone in the family on pieces of paper. Then after a fight or "just because," everyone gathers around and takes turns pulling out a slip of paper and reading the blessing. This can be especially helpful in healing hurt feelings.

The Art of Apology

Apologizing is one of the key components to conflict resolution—and one of the easiest ways to reinstate hostilities if perceived to be insincere. There's more to apologizing than saying, "I'm sorry," and we are sadly neglecting our duty as parents if we only require or expect those two words from our children. An apology has three distinct parts, each with its own significance in healing the wound.

Acknowledgment. If a child merely throws out an "I'm sorry," and scuttles back to play, it's difficult to know if she fully realizes why she had to apologize. For example, in our house, the person apologizing must state why she is sorry, as in, "I'm sorry for hitting you," rather than just, "I'm sorry." This has immensely cut down on accusations of not being sorry from the injured party and also has helped the apologizer see more clearly the consequences of her actions. This also points to what the apologizer needs to address in her own heart.

Response. The hearer of the apology has a crucial role to play as well. He shouldn't be a passive participant because he needs to truly receive the apology. We started requiring the receiver of an apology to say, "You're forgiven," as a way of reminding them both that an apology should be accepted. Then the two parties hug to make up. The physical response acts as a way to ensure the final acceptance of the apology and gives both a chance to heal. Often, such a hug will dissolve into giggles, and the pair will race off to play happily together once again.

"We always ask them to say they are sorry to each other and give the other one a hug if they have done something bad to the other child," said Elizabeth Crocker of her two- and three-year-old children. "This was hard at first, but now they do it readily when asked and even ask each other to say 'I'm sorry.'"

Restitution. Children need to be aware that at times, the apology isn't enough, that some things take time for full restitution. Once the apology has been given and received, the apologizer needs to make things right, if necessary, such as returning a toy snatched away or restoring a project to its former condition. Other times, the apologizer can't return the item because it was broken or destroyed. In that case, the apologizer may need to work out the monetary value of replacing the item, then provide the funds to that person.

Parents will need to prompt the apology and its three parts when the children are young (or if this hasn't been a practice in your home before now), but soon it will become a habit that will need a gentle prod every once in a while to continue. Don't forget to model apologizing and forgiveness to your children in your own life, especially when you have wronged them in some way. "I try to show them forgiveness, but also to ask their forgiveness if I feel like I handled something wrong," said Angela Vermilion of Aldie, Virginia.

When to Get Involved

Parents often stumble when it comes to knowing when to get involved in the fights of their offspring. The simple answer is as little as possible! Beyond the guidance to show how to resolve conflicts, when should parents get involved in sibling discord?

Blood and breakage. If the actions taken by your children have a high probability to lead to the spilling of actual blood, then step in immediately. If their roughhousing seems likely to result in something of yours being broken, then intervene. If, as is mostly the case, their high jinks are merely loud and obnoxious, there are other ways to curb that with minimal parental involvement. (The next section will give concrete ways to handle this.)

Helpless babes. When one sibling, such as an infant or toddler, is too little to be held to the same accountability standards, then you should insert yourself into the situation or remove the younger child. That isn't to say such a youngster gets a free pass on her behavior, but that the parent should be more hands-on in directing proper behavior at this age.

For the most part, parents should take giant steps back from conflict involvement to allow their offspring to figure things out on their own.

Consequences

When you have to intervene in sibling conflict, the best way to avoid playing judge is to simply punish all of them. "The kids should share in the good times as well as the bad," said Dorothy. "If my children were caught in a conflict, they were all punished. It doesn't take long for them to learn that squabbling never gets them anywhere."

To those who are crying, "That's not fair," I suggest you reread chapter 5. On the surface, this wholesale punishment reeks of unfairness, but that's because we tend to look at sibling conflict in black and white: Who started it? Who hit first? Who grabbed the toy? We want to become detectives, sniffing out clues as to who's not telling the truth, who's leaving out important information, who's in the right, and who's in the wrong. What that does is create victims and villains, which, as discussed in earlier chapters, leads to favoritism and all sorts of destructive "isms" in the family—and is guaranteed to increase sibling conflict and rivalry.

We need to look at this in a more comprehensive way and stop being narrow-minded in our view of sibling conflict. The reality is that all siblings involved in the conflict contributed to the fight in some way. You didn't see the little nitpicking the quiet older child had done for twenty minutes before the shoe flew from the hand of her little brother. You missed the pinch from the younger sibling on the tender inner arm of his older brother that triggered a shove from the couch. It's fruitless to stop and try to figure out the messy details, so skip this part entirely, leaving the unraveling of mysteries to real detectives.

❑ ❑ ❑

CONTROLLING ANGER STARTS EARLY

Why did one man attack another man over horn honking? That's the question my eleven-year-old daughter, Naomi, asked at the breakfast table after I had read a newspaper account of the incident aloud to my husband.

I started to reply that the man was simply angry, and that's why the other man was dead. Then I thought about how earlier in the week, Micah, my seven-year-old son, had gotten upset at his younger brother and walloped him in anger. Micah received punishment, but the story made me realize how important it is that parents help their children see the dangers of anger.

So I told the kids that the anger in the attacker's heart at the time was the same as in their hearts when they got upset at their siblings. That anger comes from within, and if they are not diligent in learning how to control it, it can rear its ugly head and trigger more than a punishment from Mom.

The lesson for parents is twofold. **First**, we need to help our children realize that anger is a dangerous thing, that they need to learn how to control it in childhood or it will control them their entire lives. We should deliver consequences when anger is inappropriately displayed, and talk with them about coping mechanisms when they feel angry.

Second, we need to model good examples with our own anger management. We must watch how we react to life's little annoyances, like the driver who cuts us off, the cashier who gave us the wrong change, or the mess spilled milk made on the kitchen table. When we do blow up—and we're only human, so we will have plenty of opportunities to put this into practice—we need to halt our tirades and make amends sincerely and swiftly.

By remembering that anger is merely an emotion that can be controlled, we can help equip our children so that they will be able to navigate life without having anger manage them. Of course, we can't guarantee smooth sailing, but we should do all we can to help them keep the waters calm.

❑ ❑ ❑

One small caveat: If you personally witness the entire exchange—which will be rare, if you really think about it—then you can choose to punish one or the other. This plays out in our home if I see a sibling hit another without provocation, which is very infrequent. Then the hitter only will be punished. But usually both children suffer consequences because both are guilty of creating the situation.

Remember that our goal is to have the children learn to successfully solve their own problems, leaving us free to do our grown-up things. Group punishment can provide the impetus needed for them to take conflict resolution seriously. Now before you think that group punishment will lead to one child being ganged up on by the others, read on to see how conflict is handled by the parent.

An ingenious solution is called "Do Not Disturb the Family Peace,"[1] originally proposed by family psychologist John Rosemond. Susan Slade of Los Angeles, California, encapsulated this solution perfectly: "I've taught them that if Mom gets involved, the results are never going to go in their favor."

"Do Not Disturb the Family Peace" is basically a chart form of tickets, strikes, or similar consequences. For example, our chart has the following reasons that would earn every child a ticket:

- Keep it down. (Do not become too boisterous or noisy.)
- No hurting each other. (Do not hit, punch, push, or otherwise injure your siblings.)
- No tattling. (Do not become a snitch on your siblings.)

We tacked the chart on the refrigerator with three tickets (laminated or sturdy pieces of colorful paper, like construction paper, cardboard, etc.) clipped beside it. Here's how the system works: For each time their fighting disturbs a parent's peace (and you're the judge of that—some days it will be little things and some days it will be big things), the entire group loses one ticket. If all three tickets are lost, all siblings go directly to their rooms for the rest of the day and immediately to bed after supper, lights out.

The beauty of "Do Not Disturb the Family Peace" is that the parent has little to do with the conflict itself. This eliminates the problem of trying to figure out what happened. It doesn't really matter who was at fault, does it? What this system does is put the resolution of conflict onto the children, where it belongs.

When your kids go at it hammer and tongs, simply walk in and say the magic words, "You're disturbing my peace. That's a ticket." Then you walk out and remove a ticket (or direct a child to take one) from the fridge and place it on the counter. No arguing, no drama. This keeps parents calm, cool, and collected and provides kids with a system designed to put the onus on them to get along with each other.

Each day, all three tickets are back on the fridge—no carryovers from the previous day. Some days, your kids might lose all three tickets before lunch, while other days, all will still be on the fridge after dinner. What's important is that you have a strategy for dealing with the inevitable fussiness, and that your kids are learning how to solve their own conflicts together.

Over and Done

The last piece of the conflict resolution pie is to instill in kids the concept that when it's over, it's over. "We need to teach them that when the argument is over, it is over, no grudges and no rehashing of past offenses," said Tracie of Sterling, Virginia.

Your general house rule should be that what's done and been apologized for and resolved should stay done. There should be no picking it back up and rehashing, or in the language of kids, no take backs. Nothing unravels resolution faster than when what started the fight is thrown in the doer's face again and again. We don't like it when this happens to us as adults, and children don't like it, either. We need to help them move past the conflict, not return to re-fight it on a continuous loop.

What can help keep brothers and sisters moving forward instead of backward is to remind them that their past and future are tied together. "Sometimes I have a frank conversation with them about their future. My own mother died when I was twenty-two, and my sister and I were a huge source of comfort for one another. I explain to them that this is the only sister they'll ever have, and that they need to learn how to love and respect each other and find ways to be fair and kind—even if they don't always like the other," said Cathy Martin of Ashland, Nebraska.

"My overarching approach to my daughters' relationship with one another is to tell them, repeatedly, 'You are sisters. That is a special relationship unlike any other. Your friends will come and go, but you will always be sisters,'" added Elizabeth Spencer.

Overall, remember not to get discouraged as your kids stumble and grumble through conflict resolution. They will succeed and fail, but if you stick with the principles outlined here, you will begin to see more positives than negatives. "Start with small things," advises Lynn K. of Seattle, Washington. "If you see success in the little things, that will foster the faith that it can work in bigger things as well."

❑ ❑ ❑

ADDITIONAL RESOURCES

The Brother Offended Checklist by Pam Forster shows kids what the Bible says about tattletales and what their response should be.

The Peacemaker by Ken Sande provides a wonderful overview of how to work toward peace instead of strife in your own life.

The Young Peacemaker by Corlette Sande teaches kids how to respond to conflict God's way in a variety of settings, including school.

"Siblings are the people we practice on, the people who teach us about fairness and cooperation and kindness and caring, quite often the hard way."

—Pamela Dugdale

One-on-One Time

When other parents learn we have four children, their first response is usually along the lines of "How do you juggle all those kids?" That question is generally followed by another: "How do you find time for your kids?" Both represent a misconception of how much parental time and outside activities children need. We're firm believers that children should—and are perfectly capable of—entertaining themselves. Therefore, from an early age, we provided a bit of direction and left them to their own devices. Yes, sometimes they express their boredom with the world, at which time we point them in the direction of the "chore jar." (And sometimes, that boredom does spill over into fights with siblings.) But that's not to say we don't enjoy doing things for and with our kids. Time around a board game or at the zoo can be a wonderful time of fellowship and bonding as a family.

While we don't give our kids too much attention on a daily basis, we also do not neglect to spend individual time with them apart from the family as a whole. In today's ever-busy, ever-connected world, one-on-one time with a parent becomes even more precious to a child. "We have specific activities the children picked out to do with us individually. In addition, they will sometimes get picked to go run errands alone with us or we will plan special dates to do individually with them too," said Cheri S. of Battle Creek, Michigan. "We mix it up, as in sometimes it's their day and sometimes it's mine. We take turns doing special things with each child alone."

This alone time forges a stronger bond of intimacy and love between parent and child, nourishing the relationship. Many parents recognize the importance of individual time with a child. In fact, 70 percent of the respondents to my informal sibling survey had regular one-on-one time with each of their children. "I think it's important to give both kids special time with each parent on their own and to give them space to enjoy different activities," said Elizabeth Crocker of Reston, Virginia.

Time spent alone with one child also underscores that we see them as individuals, not as a collective "the kids." We often lump our offspring all together, such as "Kids, get in the car!" It's great to be part of a family, but sometimes, children need to know we see them as single entities apart from the group. Also, having regular individual interaction will create precious memories for both of you. Group recollections are wonderful, but it's the personal touch that often brings the most pleasure to us and our kids.

Plus, all kids, especially teenagers, need that bonding time with parents, a chance to slow down and ease up on the throttle of life. "My husband and I have dates with them, but I also try to connect with each of them at bedtime or during the day with schoolwork or reading," said Angela Vermilion of Aldie, Virginia.

Research shows the significance of individual time with parents. For example, studies have found that kids need some alone time with Mom or Dad, even into the teenage years when many parents think their kids are more apt to pull away from their families. A 2012 Pennsylvania State University study discovered that children and parents spend more time together than previously thought. "Our research shows that, well into the adolescent years, teens continue to spend time with their parents and that this shared time, especially shared time with fathers, has important implications for adolescents' psychological and social adjustment," Susan McHale, director of the Social Service Research Institute at Penn State, told CNN in an interview about the study.[1] The study pointed out the benefits for children who have more family time include less aberrant behaviors and a stronger ability to withstand peer pressure.

Another advantage of individual time is the increased communication between parent and child. Parents have found that scheduled one-on-one time with their children keeps them up-to-date with what's going on in their lives. With individual time, you can cater to each child's personality and ability, which goes along with helping parents not play favorites. (See chapter 4 for more on avoiding favoritism.) Because a teenager usually doesn't enjoy the same things as an eight-year-old, family outings generally find middle ground to appeal to all ages involved. Alone time can be spent doing what interests that particular child, which can go a long way in nourishing his talents and abilities in an environment away from other siblings.

When children know they will have regular time with their parents without their siblings, they can become more tolerant and less likely to pick fights with their brothers and sisters. "I try to make each one feel important by spending time alone with each of them," said Ruth Reid of Dade City, Florida.

One final thought about the importance of one-on-one time with your children: Our time with them living at home is fleeting. We have them 24/7 for eighteen years, then they begin to spread their wings and fly to new adventures outside of our home. Sure, we may get them back occasionally, but we will never again have them at this age. So I encourage you, whatever the current ages of your children, not to be overwhelmed with the things of this life—or to allow your kids to have lives so stuffed with activities—that you don't set aside time to spend with each child individually on a regular basis.

Ground Rules

However, before you grab your calendar and start penciling in individual time with your kids, there are a few ground rules you should follow to maximize your time together—and to keep that time special. If we spend a few moments considering the how, why, and what of our outings, we will find the time with our children more meaningful.

Plan. Spontaneous outings can be fun for all involved, but deliberately setting aside time in advance—clearly marked on the family calendar—sends a message to the child that this is important to you too. It also helps us to make sure we are not accidentally overlooking one of our offspring. This is one time where planning equal time for each child is appropriate. That doesn't mean you also must reciprocate the time alone with the other children every time you run an errand with just one, or spend one-on-one time in a spontaneous situation. It does mean you make a conscious effort to include each child in your one-on-one rotations.

For example, in our family, we have "Breakfast with Mom or Dad." Here's how it works: I draw up a schedule in which on the first and third Friday mornings of each month, one child goes to breakfast with Mom or Dad, who rotate through the children. That child gets to pick the restaurant and have some alone time with a parent before school. The schedule is posted on the refrigerator, so everyone sees who's going with which parent on what date. This also helps keep cries of "It's my turn," at bay because each child can clearly see when his or her turn is coming.

Unplug. Kids know when we are not giving them our undivided attention, so don't ruin the outing by answering your phone, reading the newspaper, or surfing the Internet. Put all distractions aside and focus on your child. With a preschooler (or a teenager, come to think of it), you might not have the world's most fascinating discussion, but what you'll gain is a happier, more content kid, one who is basking in the knowledge that he is the most important person in the universe to Mom or Dad at that moment. The cost of a few missed texts is, frankly, priceless. Your child may not remember what you did that day when he's thirty, but he will remember that you took the time to truly be with him. But the reverse is also true: Your child will likely carry the hurt into adulthood from a "present in body, but absent in mind" parent during a time when Mom or Dad was supposed to be spending with him.

Talk. It's all about them, not you, not work, and definitely not their siblings! This is not the time to talk about anything else but the child in front of you. "I get time in the mornings with my son when I get up to fix breakfast. He leaves home earlier than his sister, so I see him before she comes down. With my daughter, she tends to hang out while I'm working, so quite often we talk about what we're doing on our computers and also stop what we're doing for conversations," said Mary of Owego, New York. Don't forget to pick topics that will interest them more than you. Also make it a point to listen more than you talk.

Ask. Sometimes, you'll need to get the conversation started. Open-ended questions or statements elicit the best replies. Try the following to get the ball rolling:

- Tell me something about your day.
- How do you think [insert favorite team name] will do this year?

141

- What books are you reading? Who's your favorite character?
- Who did you eat lunch with today? What did you talk about?
- How would you spend a million dollars?
- What superpower would you like to have?
- What sport would you like to play?
- What do you want to be when you grow up? Why that profession?
- What do you dream about?
- What's your favorite subject in school?

You can ask about sports, friends, TV shows, movies, music, and art. The list is endless. A bonus is that you'll probably pick up a few ideas for birthday and Christmas presents by what they like to talk about. Also ask what they like about their siblings—and what they don't. To keep it from devolving into a gripe fest, limit it to two positives and one negative. This exercise will give you a snapshot of the tenor of the household and may help to head off any major eruptions in sibling conflict.

Listen. This goes along with unplugging, but hear what your child is saying—and not saying. Read between the lines by his tone of voice, his body language, and his eye contact. Things to think about while listening include:

- Is his voice excited?
- Are his eyes downcast?
- Is he animated or dejected?
- Does he have a lot or a little to say on a particular topic?
- Does he seem anxious or relaxed?

You'll be amazed at how much you'll glean of your child's life with an individual conversation. It's a good idea to take the pulse of a child's overall well-being during these one-on-one outings, but don't overanalyze the exchange.

Share. Kids want to know about our lives as well, not the mundane stuff, but things like what you read at their age, whether or not you made the soccer team, and your favorite subject in third grade. Also tell stories about the family, like how you met their father (or mother), what they were like as a baby, what you remember most as a child in their grandparents' home, and so on. This type of family history bridges the generation gap and gives kids more of a sense of belonging. Building your shared history brings you together as a unit.

Go. These outings should be geared toward what the child wants to do, even though it might not be your first choice. Keep it on the fun side—try to avoid having all one-on-one encounters be centered around chores or errands. Those little moments in your day can be good occasions for "spot checks," that is, to check in with a child to see how things are going, but shouldn't replace one-on-one time.

For example, my eldest loves to accompany me when I grocery shop, where we talk about prices, coupons, and how to pick a ripe avocado, but we make scheduled individual time away from the usual to make it special. "I home-educated them from birth to age fifteen, so I spent part of each day learning stuff with them (often individually), reading to them, cooking, playing, and so on," said Deb Elkink of Elkwater, Alberta.

Participate. This mirrors the unplug sentiment in that you should be a full participant in the outing or event, even if you'd rather do anything other than play miniature golf or sing along to a children's band. Be a good sport and don't mope about the choice. Reach back into your own childhood to recapture the happiness you felt as a seven-year-old, or whatever the age of your child. Then use those memories to fuel your own attitude and take pleasure in the moment with your child. "We tried to get down on their level and enjoy whatever they were interested in at the time," said Cindy Damon of Fairfax, Virginia.

Overall, these ground rules are meant to be a guide as you consider how to spend one-on-one time with your children. The main takeaway point is to make the time to be with them and to have fun with your children.

Time Well Spent

It matters little what you do with your kids during your time with them, and each family's outings will reflect their interests, location, and financial situation. There are many ways you can spend time individually with your children. In my sibling survey, going to a place of the child's choosing ranked as the number-one way parents spent one-on-one time with their kids, followed by a special event and a restaurant visit. "For three years, my husband and I were able to each take a daughter out for Saturday breakfast alone. He went with one and I went with the other, according to what our schedules allowed," said Betsey Kodat of Herndon, Virginia.

❏ ❏ ❏

INDIVIDUAL TIME SNAPSHOT

The Scenario: Two of your three children seek opportunities to be alone with you, such as volunteering to come with you on errands. But the middle child doesn't speak up for these spontaneous outings. You're finding that you spend much less time with him as a result. What should you do?

The Solution: Try carving out a bit of daily interaction for just the two of you. Perhaps it's after dinner when the others are doing homework, or maybe right before bed you visit with him to check in on how his day is going. Make an effort to ask him to do something with you beyond errands, such as cook dinner or sort socks. Those little opportunities should help you stay connected with him on a more day-to-day basis.

❏ ❏ ❏

Overall, your goal should be to have an opportunity to get to know your child better, and how you do that is up to you. Don't be afraid to think outside the box for a child who might need a bit more creativity to open up. It might look different for each child and that's okay. For example, one mother started journaling back and forth with her middle son. She wrote something light and funny, plus what she saw as his strengths, in a brand-new notebook and left it on his bed. The next day, he returned the journal to her with his own thoughts. Each continued the back-and-forth journaling, ending every entry with "I love you." She met her son where he was, and the two have shared a wonderful journey together through words.

This section will list some of the things other families have done or suggested for one-on-one time with a child. This is by no means an exhaustive list of ways you can have alone time with a kid. Keep in mind that the activity is secondary to the conversation and togetherness. Look around at all the interesting things your area offers and get out there with your child. There are many resources that list kid-friendly day trips and activities, so take advantage of those as well. "Sometimes the one-on-one time becomes about the cool stuff they get to do, so we try to keep it simple," said Sharon Cartwright of Fairfax, Virginia. Sharon's advice is good to keep in mind as you plan your individual time with each of your offspring.

Books. Reading to your child should be part of every parent's repertoire, especially when the children are young. Whether it's picture books or chapter books—or even an audiobook that you listen to together—reading can be pleasurable for both of you. "Each has a special read-aloud chapter book and special snuggle time," said Alice of Vienna, Virginia. "We also play board games one-on-one and go for walks or bike rides alone. We think about what interests they share with us that their siblings might not, and that's what we do."

Car. Using travel time when you're alone with a child to catch up or chat can give you that little extra amount of time. Sometimes, kids will open up more in a car with a parent than in a face-to-face situation. Michelle Boice of Manassas, Virginia, takes advantage of any unexpected time with her kids, such as being home alone with one or in the car with one. "I talk to them or give them a special treat to show them they are loved and special," she said.

Classes. Take a class together from your local community college or city or county recreation department. From Mommy & Me for the younger set to crafts for the older kids, sharing time together doing something that interests you both can be time well spent. From languages to yoga, from cooking to karate, classes can be an easy way to have one-on-one time.

Community. Take advantage of what your community has to offer for things to do. Many of these events will be low-cost or free, and the bonus is that you may get to meet some of your children's friends and their parents in passing. For example, I've taken a child to a free, local outdoor festival, and we enjoyed looking at the craft booths together.

Games. From board games to video games, playing together can be a great way to bond (and help a child learn good sportsmanship). Try out new games, give old games new rules, or run a championship series of games. When I was about eight, my parents and I played an ongoing game of rummy one cold winter. Once or twice a week, we'd set up a small table near the woodstove and play cards for an hour, keeping a running tally until we finally ended the game in the spring.

Hobbies. Do you and a child enjoy the same hobby? Then why not do it together? Gardening, building model cars, knitting, or sewing all provide ways to bond with a child over a shared interest. Perhaps you can both learn a new craft or hobby at the same time.

Outdoors. The great outdoors is teeming with things to do, from walks in the park or along the seashore to hikes in the woods or up a mountain. You can also ride a bike, catch fireflies, watch a sunset, or count stars. The bonus for outside activities is that they usually cost very little or nothing at all, and most involve some sort of exercise.

Puzzles. Jigsaw puzzles of all levels of difficulty can provide ample opportunities for interaction between parent and child. Other puzzles, like brain teasers, can be fun as well. "I try to either read or play with each of them in some way most nights," said Elizabeth Crocker. "For example, I'll do a puzzle with my son, and then read a book just for my daughter."

Restaurants. A meal or dessert with your child could be just the ticket to unlocking communication with him. This can be an especially good outing for older children. "My kids are older, so usually when shopping with one, we will add a meal or coffee, just me and him," said Susan of Waupun, Wisconsin.

Screens. Movies, TV shows, and on-demand web shows are just a few of the visual things you can do together. Just be sure to allot time to talk about what you saw afterward to make that further connection. My husband watches a reality talent show on television with our daughters, and they chat about the format and the contestants.

Service. Is there a cause your child is passionate about? Perhaps, you two could volunteer at the local animal shelter or deliver Meals on Wheels to seniors. Doing a service project together can be a wonderful way to spend time with a child. As part of our local American Heritage Girls troop, I have the opportunity to do service projects with my girls both together and separately. That's provided a great way to see what causes or charities they want to support.

Special. Every once in a while, it's great to splurge and do something a bit more elegant than usual. A trip to the theater or a fancy restaurant meal can put a sparkle in a child's eye. Betsy DeMarco of Fairfax, Virginia, took one of her daughters to see the Nutcracker ballet and had a restaurant meal ahead of time. "I think one-on-one time with our kids is very special, even if it is just being at home with them when everyone else is out," Betsy said. "The lack of distractions makes it easy for me to notice the little things I love about the child. On their side, it can make it easier for them to open up and talk without the distractions of the sometimes-rowdy siblings. It also tells them that they are very dear to us and that we value them as an individual even if that sometimes gets lost in the everyday life of a family of six."

Sports. Whether watching or participating, sports offer a great way for a mom or dad to connect with a child. Beyond the games themselves, you can visit a local stadium for a tour or play in a fantasy league together. My husband has started to indoctrinate our oldest son into the intricacies of football through watching National Football League games together.

Talks. Just having time to chat can be golden for some kids. "When they were little, I read to them and talked to them," said Amy of Baltimore, Maryland. "I still have long talks with them to find out what their lives are like." This kind of interaction can help parents know what their children are up to on a daily basis. Jennifer Coffin of Fairfax, Virginia, added, "I sat with each one every night to talk about what went right during the day and what went wrong, and then we prayed."

Trips. These can be as simple as going to the library or bookstore, or as elaborate as a getaway weekend to mark a special occasion, such as a milestone birthday or high school or college graduation. Museums, airports, train stations, racetracks, and farms are waiting to be explored. Take a ferry or subway ride to the end of the line and back again.

Silly or serious, activities can generate many opportunities for making warm memories. Sometimes, we think it has to be big to be memorable, but that's usually not the case. For more ideas, ask your parents what you did with them as a child. Some of my fondest memories are the little things I did with my parents, such as walking in the warm summer rain with my mother or sanding wood in the basement workshop with my father. Don't discount those little slivers of time that you spend one-on-one with your child. You might find one day that those were some of the best times in his or her growing up years.

Also don't forget to have fun together as a family. Building that camaraderie forges strong links that will hold the brothers and sisters together during rocky times. Sometimes you might want to split up the family, such as all the boys going out with Dad while the girls do something with Mom. And don't sweat the financial outlay for these "dates" because you can make it work to fit any budget, from nonexistent to upscale. The most important element is face time with a parent.

Working something else into your schedule might seem daunting, but the payoff and the personal time is worth the effort. You could start out with once a month and go from there— just scheduling the dates shows how important you view your child. The follow-through with the outing can be priceless. "We take each kid to the mall, park, or restaurant alone every month or two," said Christina Tarabochia of Tigard, Oregon.

Above all, remember the first half of Psalm 127:3: "Behold, children are a heritage from the LORD." We should enjoy that legacy here and now. We should not let the chance to develop more meaningful relationships with our kids slip away. Take the first small steps to make one-on-one time with your children a priority today.

"We are not only our brother's keeper;
in countless large and small ways,
we are our brother's maker."

—Bonaro Overstreet

Breathing Room

Ever notice that being trapped inside for several days because of weather or sickness can unleash the worst behavior from our children? While the family members that play together do indeed develop a deeper relationship with each other, too much togetherness can breed undesirable behaviors. Time away from other siblings can provide a much-needed respite and can prevent tensions from reaching the boiling point and exploding into conflict.

Just as we parents need to ensure we spend time together as a family, so we should encourage time apart. Everyone, from Mom and Dad on down to the youngest child, needs alone time—the trick is finding the right balance to avoid both smothering (too much togetherness) and becoming antisocial (too much time alone). "I have to send them each to their own space," said Mary of Owego, New York. "They spend a lot of time together, and sometimes need a reminder to separate and give each other room."

It's important that we talk with our children about why time alone is good for everyone, and that it shouldn't always be viewed as a punishment. We all feel so busy these days, overwhelmed by our lengthy and never-ending to-do lists. Busyness has become a status symbol as we're always rushing around from one task to another, on the job 24/7. We fill our lives with constant motion and tasks to be accomplished. Even Christians fall into the trap of over-scheduling, overdoing, and over-committing our time and resources. Our children are not any different, with over-packed schedules and constant motion, leaving little time for the business of being a kid.

Jesus' words in Matthew 11:28—"Come to me, all who labor and are heavy laden, and I will give you rest"—is such a text for any age, but if it ever had resonance, poignancy, and pointedness, it is our age because heaviness and weariness define most people in our day and age. As adults, we know that time alone can rejuvenate, restore, and revive us. This is a lesson even our children can learn as we help them discover the joys and restorative powers of being by themselves. "We talk to our kids about giving each other time to themselves, to calm down, to refocus, and to reassess their actions, their duties, and their hearts," said Jacqui Rapp of Fairdale, Kentucky.

Alone time has two components: knowing when to separate and having a place to be alone. Therefore, to accomplish the appropriate ratio of togetherness and separateness, parents should first figure out when a separation is necessary. Part of this step is training offspring to recognize their personal warning signs so that they can remove themselves from a potentially explosive situation. Second, parents need to help children find private space in the home for alone time. Coupled with finding privacy is parents' duty to assist their children to have their own identity within the family unit, another form of separating. This chapter will discuss both how to know when a volcano might erupt and how to create space for the essential cool-down period.

Before the Storm

We know that hindsight can provide a clearer picture of what went wrong in a fight, but it also can give parents essential clues as to what triggers some of the sibling conflict in their family. If you think back on a recent squabble between your kids, you will likely be able to pinpoint when things started breaking down. While there are as many reasons for fights as there are children, here are some common sparks that can escalate into sibling friction.

Anticipation. The days and hours before an event, such as Christmas, a birthday, school test, or sports game, can be a time of wonder and expectation. But at the same time, it can raise the tension level among siblings to new heights.

In our home, one child (who will remain nameless for this example) becomes a bit hyper prior to a longed-for occasion. This child will pick on younger and older siblings, bother a brother or sister, and generally become a nuisance. Knowing this child's predilection for being a pest when something out of the ordinary is going to happen puts my husband and me on high alert during those times. We head off any major run-ins by encouraging outside play and/or separate activities. This has greatly reduced the number of sibling fights related to this particular child's excitement.

We remind this child in the days leading up to a special event of the child's tendency to pick on the others, and this child often voluntarily finds ways to be alone. We also encourage the other kids to give the child a wider berth—and more understanding at these times. You also can use a buzzword, as discussed in an earlier chapter, to alert the child that his or her behavior might be edging toward crossing a line into conflict.

Frustration. Frustration can be another way sibling clashes start. Children express their frustration in different ways, some turning inward and some lashing outward. Keep in mind that some kids don't wear their frustration on their sleeves, but instead are more devious in expressing it, turning the screws behind the scenes of sibling rivalry. Knowing how your children react to frustration can provide clues as to when you need to separate them.

"When they really seem to be intolerant of each other, I force a separation," said Cathy Martin of Ashland, Nebraska. "I don't necessarily discipline them with the separation. I will make them go to their separate rooms or play in totally different areas, such as one on the computer downstairs and one watching TV or reading upstairs. When we get to this point, I explain that since they cannot be kind to one another, they don't get to play with each other."

As frustration can be aimed at themselves or at a sibling, parents can help their children to see how they react. For example, when you see a child becoming frustrated on a regular basis with her homework, have that child move from the kitchen table to a quieter place to complete the assignment. That will address her anxiety and limit her access to siblings, thus reducing some of the potential for conflict. Reminding that child of her tendency to become frustrated while doing homework can help her to know when to voluntarily remove herself in the future to a more secluded spot.

Differences. Our children are all unique human beings. These differences also mean that separation can be a positive thing at times. One of the most overlooked variances that can cause conflict among siblings is age. Older kids don't want to do what younger ones do, and younger children find older kids too mature. Not forcing too many activities together for disparate ages can lessen tensions.

However, mixing up the ages also can alleviate some mash-ups among brothers and sisters. For example, I'll suggest pairings of my four kids that separate the closest in age, such as the oldest girl with the oldest boy, to lower the stress level. When you know who's more likely to not get along among your kids, it's easier to divide them up for maximum peace. "When tensions are rising, I simply send them to separate areas. That may be one reading, one playing outside, one in the playroom, etc. I send them off to work on things that make them happy," said Meghan of Arlington, Virginia.

Gender can be another sore spot, especially if you have more of one gender than another. Boys and girls play differently, think differently, and engage with the world differently. Sure, there is a crossover appeal for some things, but neglecting to let boys be boys and girls be girls at times can factor into sibling fights. For example, with two girls and two boys in my house, I sometimes remind the older girls that their younger brothers play loudly not to annoy their sisters but because they're boys.

Temperaments are another difference among siblings. Some kids like to be still and quiet, while others enjoy getting physical and noisy. Knowing which child is which type can be essential to managing the expectations of other siblings. For instance, one of my cousins, very close in age to me and like a sister, had tons more energy as a child than I did. Some of our biggest fights happened because she wanted to go, go, go, while I wanted to stay still and read. We eventually figured out how to compromise on our activities so that we both enjoyed them.

Make your kids aware of these differences by talking about them, along with ways to relate to them in the family. For instance, you can point out how some siblings enjoy building things while others like to race scooters down the sidewalk. You could share some stories from your own childhood that illustrate this point and how you worked together with the person to your mutual satisfaction. That could cut down on the more active children constantly hounding the more sedate ones—and thus upping the friction among brothers and sisters.

Health. Sick or tired kids can be cranky children. When ill, exhausted, or not at their best physically, children can have frayed tempers and an increased likelihood of becoming stormy. Some children lash out more easily when tired, while others get snappish when they have a cold. Noticing a tired kid before the meltdown can circumvent sibling clashes. Telling a sibling that a child is ill also can help the sibling react with more compassion to behavior that, under normal circumstances, would not be viewed as charitably. Just as we're more likely to overlook offenses when our spouse has the flu, so can children try harder to ignore annoyances from a sibling who is sick.

We can assist in this more sympathetic attitude by engaging the well siblings in service to the sick child, such as reading to her or bringing her tissues. This also helps them have a more servant-like heart toward their sibling. One note of caution: For a special needs or chronically ill child, take care that the siblings are not forced to constantly adhere to that child's limitations.

When you notice atypical behavior that grates on a sibling's nerves, you might want to consider what's contributing to the problem—not to exclude the actions, but to head off an even bigger explosion through some judicious separation maneuvers. "I make sure they have a safe zone to go to where they can calm down and rethink about what has happened. I also make sure they understand why they need their own space so they respect each other's need for space. I also encourage their interests and allow them to do things that are separate from the others," said Michelle Boice of Manassas, Virginia. Our goal should be to keep an eye out to circumstances that could contribute to sibling upheaval and to separate the children before or at the start of potential hostilities.

A Place of Their Own

Essential to any calm household is a place for each person to be alone, even for a few minutes. The larger your family—and the smaller your home—the greater the challenge, but there are many creative ideas to make this work for all families. "To the extent possible, they had their own space, their own bedrooms, their own friends, their own possessions, and their own projects," said Betsey Kodat of Herndon, Virginia.

This underlines the most important aspect of private space—that it will look different in each family because of the number of children, the number of bedrooms, the way of life, and the overall size of the house. The most important aspect of this isn't how big the space is but that you are taking seriously their need for alone time and space. There are several ways for children to have a place to themselves—even in homes where they share bedrooms or space is at a premium.

Having their own bedroom. The most obvious private space is a bedroom to oneself. This is the easiest way to create a personal area for kids. "They each have their own bedrooms, which we've made special for each of them and given them permission to get away from everyone there. We also encourage finding space all their own to unwind in other parts of the house," said Tiffany Amber Stockton of Colorado Springs, Colorado.

If you live in a house with space for separate bedrooms, make the bedroom off-limits to other siblings. Allow the bedroom's "owner" to restrict access to the room for other siblings. Enforce this rule when necessary, as respecting each other's privacy is a huge component of sibling harmony.

However, with kids having their own bedroom, a few caveats are in order to keep the family peace.

- Don't allow a child to hide another's things in her room, as this can create a whole host of problems.
- Don't let the room become an escape from family time.
- Don't let the child keep the room as messy as she wants.
- Don't let the child block all access to her room all the time.

Shared bedrooms. In many homes with multiple children, bedrooms house more than one child, generally siblings of the same sex. If, like in my own home, children share bedrooms, there are ways to carve out separate space within the rooms themselves. For instance, "We allow one child at a time in the bedroom by himself to read, play, etc.," said Karen of Milford, Delaware.

Within the confines of the room, you can help children to have their own areas. For example, make each bed like a mini-island for that child. The other children shouldn't take anything—or even sit on the bed—without the child's permission. Your kids can use their imaginations to create personal space, such as hanging a blanket to turn a lower bunk bed into an instant "cave." Turn an unused corner into a study area with a beanbag, lap desk, and clip-on lamp.

Make sure you have enough storage for the children inside the room. Wall pockets, separate dressers or drawers, under-the-bed storage, or over-the-door storage can provide each child with enough personal space to store their treasures, school supplies, shoes, and clothing. Also, shelves on the wall or in a bookcase can be divided among the room's occupants if necessary. Lockboxes can provide secure storage for older kids who want to keep their valuables safe from younger siblings.

Above all, make respect of another's property a top priority. Inform siblings that destroying or stealing another's things will not be tolerated. Encourage an open-hand policy in regards to sharing their things, but respect the right of the child to hold some items as sacred to her alone. This will help the children to stay out of their siblings' treasures—and thus not cause more sibling conflict over things.

House space. Most homes have unused or rarely accessed space that can be allocated for personal use. Help your kids find space within your house to use for alone time. "We try to carve out space for our oldest son to read alone by finding a quiet space for him outside of his room," said Sharon Cartwright of Fairfax, Virginia.

Remember that kids don't need a lot of space and often love to be tucked away into nooks and crannies. Walk through the house with an eye toward finding areas that could be retrofitted for one or two children. Have your children make suggestions as to where they could have some private space, and then work with them to modify those areas.

For example, with a beanbag chair and a lamp, a small corner could become a reading nook. The large closet in the guest room could hold a small table and stool for puzzles or crafts. The second-floor landing could house a chair and laptop stand. For other ideas, check out one of the home-improvement television shows or books, or visit Pinterest.

All in the family. In today's super-sensitive child-rearing environment, parents often forget that a family doesn't need to live in each other's pockets to have close and healthy relationships. It's perfectly fine for some outings to be attended by all, some to have just one parent and a few of the kids, or some with just the children together or in various combinations.

One way to avoid too much familiarity is not to require every child to participate in every family outing. Do things as a family, but also allow for times of separation from the family to stem the flow of any bad feelings created because of too much togetherness. "We don't force everyone to participate in whole family activities all the time to give our kids breathing room," said Jane Thompson of Sarasota, Florida.

Individual activities. While it might be easier for all the kids to play the same sport, it might be unwise if the other children don't particularly like that sport. Instead, encourage kids to develop their own interests apart from their siblings. "The two boys have separate interests, such as choir versus baseball, and we encourage that," said Charles Gluck of Herndon, Virginia. "Our kids take time on their own to do their own thing," added Kerry of Webster, Massachusetts. "One is a LEGO builder, the other a racetrack engineer."

Separate activities—whether athletic, musical, artistic, or play—can help alleviate competition among siblings. Kids can forge their own identities apart from their brothers and sisters through different areas of interest. (See chapter 3 on how this can help families avoid sibling competition.)

Forced separation. Many times, kids don't realize they need time apart. That's when parents will need to forcibly separate the kids. "I send some to different ends of the house, or outside so they aren't in each other's space all the time," said Lucy Morgan-Jones of Boort, Victoria, Australia, of her four children.

This can act as a cool-down period for heated tempers and also can make playtime together go more smoothly in the future. Sometimes, parents can accomplish this by allowing them to participate in a similar activity separately. "Sometimes, I put separate movies on in different rooms for them," said Cheryl Harnden of McLean, Virginia. Personally, I'll often suggest a child do something else when I see tempers begin to flare. This method has cut down on full-blown conflict eruptions in our household.

Rest time. Many parents use a regular quiet time for all ages, including teenagers, to keep tempers on an even keel. Brandi Dixon of Birmingham, Alabama, recommended "separate 'thinking' times" as a good way to give her kids breathing room. Younger kids generally nap during this time, but older kids could read, play games, or any other quiet activity in their rooms for a specific amount of time. On days when our kids are crankier than usual, we enforce a room time for an hour or so. Some days, they don't want to come out when their hour is up because they are playing so nicely. For kids who can't read a clock, set a kitchen timer to avoid premature queries as to the end of rest time.

Play dates. In a quest for fairness, some parents insist that any invitation extended to one child must include all siblings, or at least the ones closest in age to the invited brother or sister. This can do more harm than good when it comes to sibling harmony. Children should be allowed to have time with a friend without a brother or sister tagging along. Separate play dates can give a child breathing room too. We encourage this by allowing one child at a time to invite a friend over. "We let our kids have play dates with other kids alone," said Alice of Vienna, Virginia. "This is an issue for us, as my boys are close in age. However much they like to play together or with a group, they also need time alone with a good buddy."

❏ ❏ ❏

SEPARATION SNAPSHOT

The Scenario: Your two daughters ages eight and six play together nicely, but when their two cousins who are similar ages come over, it's bedlam. Within half an hour, your youngest will be crying over being excluded by her older sister from the games or play. You constantly have to intervene to keep any semblance of peace. What can you do?

The Solution: In this case, ignoring the problem or letting the children figure it out themselves is not likely to work. Things have gone too far and their "positions" have become so entrenched that they can't change on their own. Nor can you act as mediator—you've seen how successful that's been! Here's a way to handle this. The next time the cousins are scheduled to come over, have your daughters draw straws or flip a coin to determine which one of them will get to play with the cousins. The other child will stay away from the cousins and get her turn next time it's play-time with the cousins. You'll likely have to do this for the next four or so times the cousins are at your house before you can ask your two daughters if one of them needs to play separately from the rest. This puts the onus of figuring out how to get along on the shoulders of your daughters, where it belongs.

Overall, look for simple ways to create breathing room by encouraging or forcing separations before tempers ignite, and by providing physical and emotional space within the family and the house. "I encourage them to find a place apart from each other to do something new that doesn't involve the other," said Julie Arduini of Youngstown, Ohio. Separation—whether by space or activity—can be a very positive way to curtail sibling conflict and one that most families will find works well.

"I don't believe an accident of birth makes people sisters or brothers. It makes them siblings, gives them mutuality of parentage. Sisterhood and brotherhood is a condition people have to work at."

—Maya Angelou

Introducing New Siblings

A child can become a sibling in several ways—through the birth of a brother or sister, through the adoption of a baby or older child, or through the remarriage of a parent to a spouse with children. However that sibling comes along, the child's world changes dramatically. Sometimes, the transition is accompanied by resentment and misbehavior by the former singleton, but parents can ease the transition from an only to a sibling. For ease of explanations, I'll refer to families growing from one child to two in this chapter, but these ideas and suggestions can easily apply to any size family that's adding a new baby or child to its members.

In our home, we welcomed our second child when our firstborn was twenty-two months old. Naomi, the older daughter, adjusted fairly well to her new little sister, Leah—or so we thought until the day Naomi announced very loudly that I needed to "put Leah down, just put her down," accompanied by vehement hand motions. That clued us in that Naomi wasn't taking the addition of a sibling as well as we had initially hoped.

However, that rather rocky beginning hasn't meant an escalation of hostilities between the pair. Instead, as we showed Naomi how to interact with her sister—and as Leah grew older and more able to play with her older sister—the two of them have become good friends as well as sisters, despite occasional squabbles.

Helping an older child learn to accept and love a younger sibling can be accomplished fairly easily as long as the parents don't overreact to the situation and train the older one to relate to the younger one. Children are resilient beings, capable of readjusting expectations to new circumstances fairly easily. With guidance, parents can use that ability to swing the older children into acceptance and love for their new siblings.

A New Baby

The birth of a baby is a joyous occasion, one to be celebrated, but one that can create trepidation in the hearts of mothers who fear their older child will not respond well to a new brother or sister. Many moms and dads worry about the older child feeling "deserted." They may also feel they won't have enough time for the child when the new baby arrives. Part of their concern centers around the fear they have that the older child will experience negative reactions to the young sibling.

All parents experience some of those concerns at one time or another, but it's good to remember that it's not our job to ensure the older child won't be jealous, angry, or frustrated by a new sibling—those feelings are inevitable in any person's or child's life. What parents can and should do is to give the older child assistance in adjusting to his or her new role as a big brother or big sister. Here are some ways to smooth the arrival of a new baby.

❑ ❑ ❑

ADJUSTMENT SNAPSHOT

The Scenario: Your three-year-old child has suddenly become very difficult in the weeks after you came home from the hospital with a new baby sister. He ignores your commands, laughs when punished, and has had numerous potty "accidents." You're wondering if the new sibling has created a three-year-old monster. Will his behavior improve on its own or should you intervene now?

The Solution: The birth of a sibling—as with any major event in a child's life—can throw the older child into a tizzy. Regressions are a typical response and will pass with gentle encouragement and consistency on your part. First, don't reassure him with words but actions as to his place in the family. With everyone oohing and aahing over the baby, he's feeling a bit left out. Start by setting aside some time just for him each day. Ask for his help in sorting clothes. While you're feeding the baby, sing some songs with him or read him a story. As much as you can, ignore his attitude and work on correcting his behaviors. Remind him that he knows how to use the toilet but has forgotten. Show him how to clean up after his "on purposes" and rinse out his underwear. Be matter of fact but firm, and he should return to his usual self in a few weeks.

Before the baby comes home, have realistic expectations of what life will be like. You won't be able to provide instructions ahead of time to the older sibling for all the contingencies that will happen once the new baby is home. Do what you can, but know you can't cover every possibility—and then don't sweat it. Children have become siblings since time began, and it's not always been a traumatic occurrence.

During your pregnancy, share age-appropriate details about the baby. Be open to questions about the baby and his arrival, making sure to answer the question being asked—not the one you think you heard. Many times, children are being very literal with their queries or have a totally different idea in mind than we would think, so probe a bit before tackling the answer to ensure you're on the same page. Discuss any fears or worries the child may have about having another human being in the home. Common questions include, "Where will the baby sleep?" and "Will you and Daddy still love me when the baby's born?"

To help make the baby more real, ask your child to help you get ready for the infant's arrival by preparing the baby's room. A toddler can stack diapers, while a preschooler can sort baby board books. Older children can assist with painting, assembling the crib, and putting away baby clothes. Involving the children in the preparation process also gives them "buy-in" to the baby's arrival. Do remind the child that the baby will cry and sleep a lot when he first comes home. This can prepare the child for the boredom of babyhood, at least as it will be seen from her perspective.

Decide who will care for your child during the delivery, and let the child know the plan well in advance. If it will be with someone the child doesn't see regularly, try Skyping or other forms of communication to put the child more at ease with the relative or friend. If possible, have the person come stay with you a few days before the baby's due date. If the child will be staying at someone else's house, have her pack a to-go bag like the one you'll be taking to the hospital or birthing center. Be sure to include her favorite stuffed toy or security blanket so she will feel safe while you're away.

Once the baby is born, have your husband bring the child to the hospital to visit you and the baby, if possible. If not, call the older child or video-conference her on your cell phone so that she can see you and her new sibling. Help the new baby "introduce" himself to your older child, such as saying, "Peter, meet your big sister, Anna." Some parents also have the baby "give" the older sibling a small gift.

When you come home with the new baby, give your child time to get acquainted with her brother or sister. Don't expect the child to go googly-eyed over the newborn. Despite your preparation, she's probably expecting more than a red-faced, crying baby who takes up more of your time than she antici-pated. Give the older child space to develop her own opinion of the baby.

In general, there are some things you could do to help the older child become more accepting of the baby. Do encourage her to help you care for the newborn. She can bring you diapers, blankets, pacifiers, and burp cloths. She can rock the baby in a swing or cradle, watch the baby on the floor, and pat the baby's hands when the baby fusses.

Do include the older child in the baby's routines, such as reading to her sometimes when you're nursing the baby or sing-ing silly songs while you're changing the baby's diaper. Those little touches can make an older child feel more connected to both you and the baby.

Do give the older child one-on-one attention each day. Even five minutes of snuggle time without the baby can be enough to show the child her mommy hasn't forgotten her. But don't be overly concerned if some days you can't manage even that be-cause you're too tired or the baby fussed all day.

Do ask your husband to spend a bit more time with the old-er child, such as reading her a story before bed or letting her help him with the household chores. This also is a great way for a dad to feel helpful and connected since the majority of an infant's care tends to fall on the mom.

Do show the older child how to interact with the baby, such as where she can touch him, how to hold him, and what to give him or not give him. Be patient as the child learns to be gentle.

Remember that with a toddler or preschooler, you'll have to repeat the instructions often.

Do expect some regression from the older child. Some children start sucking thumbs again, wanting a bottle, or carrying around a blanket when a newborn arrives at home. This phase will not last forever, so don't worry about the infantile behavior. To curb some of those tendencies, remind the older child of what she can do that the baby can't, such as ride a bike, eat ice cream, and not take as many naps.

Do remind her of her own special place in the family. With everyone oohing and ahhing over the baby, an older child can feel left out. Telling her from time to time what makes her unique, such as her position as firstborn or her sparkly blue eyes, will help her remember that she is loved. You should also talk to her about all the things she will be able to show the baby one day—how to tie shoes, read a book, or play Go Fish.

Do keep as much of the family routine in place as possible. Children thrive on sameness, so strive to have the days go as much according to the former schedule as you can with a newborn at home. Also, try not to forget any promised activities or other important events. (Make it a point to record those things or help the child to do so on the family calendar to assist in remembering.)

Do encourage empathy from the older child. Help the child to see the baby as a real human being, one with feelings and emotions all his own. Say things like, "See how he smiles when you talk to him," and "Your singing made him stop crying." These exchanges encourage the child to connect with the infant.

There are also some things you should try not to do when a new baby comes home. Don't expect perfection from the older child. She will melt down at times because of your attention to the baby. She will become whiny and cranky when the baby's presence means a restriction on the older child's lifestyle. Those are all normal things, so don't worry much when they happen.

Don't tell your child that she can play with the new sibling, as this scenario is far into the future. Instead, show her what she can do now, such as bounce him gently in his bouncy seat or shake a rattle for him to watch.

Don't use the baby as an excuse. Instead of saying, "We'll go to the park when the baby is awake," tell your child, "We'll go to the park after lunch." Not tying everything to the baby will help the older child see the baby's proper place as part of the family, not its sole occupant.

Don't leave a young child alone with the baby. It's too much responsibility for a youngster to know how to act around a baby, so make sure the two are not unsupervised. How old a child should be to be alone with a baby depends on the child, so if you're unsure, then keep an eye on the child with the infant. For older children, remember not to use them too often as babysitters. Give them time to merely be the big sister and not the caregiver.

Don't make it all about the baby. Yes, the baby is the cutest infant in the whole wide world, but that doesn't mean you have to coo over him every second of every day. Keep some of those moments behind closed doors or when your child is in bed or away from home. This will temper the flames of jealously in the older child.

Don't require silence when the baby sleeps. Newborns can generally sleep through anything, and while you can request the noise to be toned down, don't worry about eliminating it entirely. Babies who learn to sleep through some background hubbub are generally better sleepers, so your child should play as normally as possible while the baby naps.

Don't yell at the child for doing something wrong with the baby. In other words, as long as the baby is not in immediate, physical danger, try to hold back. For example, when our third child, Micah, was just a few weeks old, he was resting in his bouncy chair while I made dinner in the kitchen a few steps away. His older sister, Leah, who was two-and-a-half at the time, stood close by watching him. Suddenly, she bent down, placed her hands on either side of his head, and lifted him up before letting go. Thankfully, the bouncy chair did what it was supposed to do and bounced him gently. Rather than scold her, I instead asked her why she did that. Her reply? "I thought he wanted to be lifted up by his ears like Uncle Scott did to us." It took me a while to parse out that she meant the trick my older brother did by "lifting" her up by the ears when she was standing. I chuckled and told Leah that Micah was too little to enjoy that trick.

Don't push sibling bonding. Avoid urging the older child into contact with the baby. Most kids will eventually come around and show interest in the baby, but they usually want to do that on their own terms.

Overall, remember that while you and your husband have been anticipating the newborn's arrival for a long time, your child may not have been as excited. Add to that the baby probably isn't quite what she expected, plus the changes to the household, and it's no wonder that most kids aren't thrilled with a new sibling at first. But don't fret over setbacks or outbursts from the older child. Give it time and she will settle down and accept—and indeed embrace—her new status as a big sister.

Adoption

Adoption is different from birth only in that you might have a longer or shorter wait—and the new sibling might be an infant or an older child. Much of the same dos and don'ts discussed in the preceding chapter apply to the arrival of a newly adopted baby. However, there are a few differences. Let's start with the positives.

Do let your kids know that you're pursuing adoption. Be careful about imparting too much information. With the little ones you might want to wait until you're further along in the process, but do not spring it on them at the last minute.

Do tell her that it's your decision to adopt—yours and your spouse's—not hers. The child might have begged for a sibling, but that doesn't mean she's responsible for the decision. This is important because the child might come to feel jealous or to resent the newcomer—feelings that are typical when a new baby arrives through birth. If the child thinks she was the reason for the adoption, this might confuse her.

Do encourage the child to ask questions and share her feelings about the adoption and the process. Welcoming another child into the home, especially an older one, can trigger concerns and worries, such as, "Will my parents give me up?" and "What if I lose my mommy and daddy?" Many Christian parents use the analogy of how we're all God's adoptive children as a way to explain adoption.

Do let the child know the adopted baby is as much a part of the family as she is. Discourage talk along the lines of "You aren't my real brother and sister." Emphasize that families are made differently, and that adoption is one of those ways. What matters in the end is that everyone is part of the same family.

Do remember that you, as a parent, will love and relate to an adopted child differently from your biological child *much in the same way you would react differently to a biological second child.* As mentioned previously in this book, all children are different, and that means we relate to them in ways that are unique to our relationship with them. That doesn't mean we love them any less, but we do love them all uniquely because they are their own, separate people. So if you question your feelings about the adopted child, as in, "Do I feel differently about him because he's adopted?" or reactions to the child, as in, "Would I react this way with a biological child?", remind yourself that you would be thinking similar thoughts if the child had come into your family through biology instead of adoption.

Do prepare all your children for questions from strangers about their heritage, especially if you adopt children from another country or culture. Role-play with your kids on how to handle the at times insensitive or downright rude questions and statements strangers, relatives, schoolmates, or friends ask of an adopted child or his siblings.

Do work with both children to recognize their common ground, especially with an older adopted child. Much as you guide some of the interactions among biological siblings, you must do so between adopted and biological siblings. Remember that the issues will be the same for both.

Do expect dust-ups between the adopted child and the biological child. When the biological child shouts that he wishes the other kid had never been adopted, don't overreact—that's akin to saying "I hate you" or "I wish you were dead" among biological siblings. Nearly all siblings have times of frustration like this.

There are a few things to watch out for when adopting a child into your family. Don't overly emphasize the differences between the adoptive child and the biological one. If the child is from another country or culture, the differences might be physical and stark. But keep in mind that you are a family, and as such need to function as a unit. Making too much of a child's "otherness" or heritage could foster feelings of envy or jealously among the other children—or it could make the adoptive child feel like an outsider in the family.

Don't expect the biological child to do too much for the adopted child. In the case where the adopted child is not an infant but of an age with the biological child, take care not to rely on the biological child to help assimilate the adopted child into school, church, social circles, and extended family life. Remember that your first child is trying to adjust to having a sibling much as the adopted child is figuring out how to fit into your family.

Overall, do remember that just because a child is adopted doesn't mean that he should be treated differently from biological children. The kids will fight, argue, and behave badly toward one another, but they will also love, cherish, and laugh together too.

Yours, Mine, and Ours

When a parent remarries another parent, the children of both often find themselves thrown together in living situations. But there's hope for a smooth relationship between the two families. When blending a family, here are some things to keep in mind.

Do tell the children that you expect them to learn how to be around each other, whether it's for a vacation, weekend visits, or a full-time living together situation. Just like brothers and sisters who live together all the time must find a way to coexist peacefully, so should kids brought together by their parents' marriage.

Do expect jealousy from your children if their stepbrothers and stepsisters receive pricier gifts or fancy electronics from the other parent. But don't try to keep up with the other parent by purchasing similar presents for your kids. That will only fuel the flames of competition and rivalry. Instead, focus on helping your children overcome their envy.

Do talk with the other parent to ensure discipline, expectations, and other issues are as close to being the same in both households as possible. Depending on the acrimony a divorce might have triggered, this might not be realistic, but you should continue to try to make the adjustments the kids make from your home to the other home as smooth as possible.

Do expect misbehavior when your stepchildren return from a visit to the other parent's home. Much like my own children are usually not on their best behavior when they return from a week at their grandparents' home, stepchildren coming back from vacation, a weekend visit, or lengthy time with the other parent can exhibit less-than-desirable behaviors. This would be a good time to employ some of the breathing room strategies we discussed in chapter 9.

Do keep separate bedrooms for each gender (boys with boys, girls with girls). If they must share rooms, try to employ some of the ideas from the last chapter pertaining to storage and personal space.

Do treat stepchildren as your own children. They might not call you Mom or Dad, but they should be treated as your own offspring. This means in all areas—discipline, chores, and privileges.

Do realize your children might take a bit longer to get over the hurt of a divorce or death of a parent. Seeing a parent re-marry could trigger feelings that they might have thought had been healed. The children may have been fine with their parent "moving on" in theory, but the reality of a new Mom or Dad could bring about a return of grief or even guilt for loving someone else.

Do continue with one-on-one time with your biological children and your stepchildren. By including the stepchildren in the mix, you'll get to know them better. This also might head off any potential blowups if they see you treat them the same.

Do make some new traditions, especially around the holidays. One of the best ways to accomplish this is to ask the children individually what they like best about Christmas, for example. Then call a family meeting to talk about how to incorporate some of everything on the list. You could make a rule that each family contributes one "tradition" for each holiday, and then you come up with a new one that fits the blended family.

Do apply house rules to all children in the house, even if they're only at home on the weekends. Making exceptions for "weekend visitors" will only create bad feelings among the siblings who are at home during the week.

Now let's discuss some of the things best avoided in order to establish a more harmonious home.

Don't try to be fair. As we've discussed in chapter 5, fairness rarely works, so while it might be very tempting to make sure your kids and your stepchildren are equally treated, there will still be perceptions of unfairness. Instead, focus on each child's uniqueness and place in the family—you'll find things go much easier with that attitude.

Don't expect too much. Most blended families aren't ready to become the Brady Bunch overnight—and some never achieve that level of harmony. You can expect a "honeymoon" period that could lull you into thinking everything's okay. Go slowly with the integration, and realize that sibling rivalries might surface later as the children adjust to one another.

Don't expect the children to love each other as much as you love your new spouse. Most of the time, the two parents wait to introduce their kids to one another and probably limit the time those kids spent together. Therefore, the children still have to get to know their new siblings, and that takes time and effort.

Don't change everything at once. As with traditions, you can keep some of the routines from each family by compromising a bit to accommodate both families. For example, if one set of kids enjoys having a full breakfast at eight every Saturday morning, but the second set would rather sleep in later, move the meal to nine or ten to split the difference.

Don't issue ultimatums. You don't want to get into situations where you feel you have to choose between your kids and your stepchildren. Work toward solutions that encompass everyone, not ones that benefit one set of kids over the other.

With more than twelve million kids age eighteen and younger living in blended homes,[1] this way of building a family has become more commonplace. But with a little forethought, you can guide your kids and your spouse's children toward becoming, if not fast friends, at least not hostile enemies.

There might be some different rough patches to navigate, but keep pressing on with the principles and suggestions in this book, and you'll find that siblings, no matter how they come to be part of the family, interact in basically the same way.

"Our siblings push buttons that cast us in roles we felt sure we had let go of long ago— the baby, the peacekeeper, the caretaker, the avoider. . . . It doesn't seem to matter how much time has elapsed or how far we've traveled."

—Jane Mersky Leder

Conclusion

Children are a blessing from God. Having more than one child has its own set of challenges, but sibling rivalry doesn't have to be one of them. Relationships are messy, and sibling interactions are among some of the messiest relationships on earth. It's unrealistic for parents to expect their kids to get along perfectly all the time. What we can hope is for them to develop a heart that repents for wrongdoing and strives to serve others.

Brothers and sisters provide one another with memory banks of shared laughter and heartache, forming a strong bond that transcends the often rough-and-tumble play of childhood. Of course, not all siblings will grow up to be best friends, but with care, we can at least provide them with the tools and encouragement to become friends. We might worry that their fighting will lead to a lifetime of animosity, but families do testify that the fights of childhood dissipate when the children are adults.

Overall, we should focus on equipping them with the tools to resolve conflict because these are the skills that will be beneficial to them throughout their lives. What we should remember is that, in most families, the fights of childhood—if resolved in real time—usually dissolve in adulthood. One study conducted by Dr. Victoria Bedford at the University of Indianapolis found that while 75 percent of respondents fought with brothers and sisters "somewhat" or "extremely" frequently as kids, 87 percent of those siblings said that arguments with their brothers and sisters happened "hardly ever or not at all" as adults. In addition, around 80 percent of brothers and sisters who experienced fights in childhood said they used those skills to resolve conflict positively in adulthood.[1]

However, parents should keep in mind that the sibling bond isn't indestructible, that resentment, favoritism, and competition can derail the relationship, sometimes permanently. But parents also must remember that we are not the only ones responsible for the relationships of our children—they, too, have a responsibility for getting along with one another, for thinking the best of a brother or sister instead of the worst, for building each other up rather than tearing each other down, and for learning to resolve fights in a manner that's respectful to all involved. Our kids are fully capable of figuring this out, with some assistance from us.

The last thing to consider is that we need to focus more on what's important—the hearts of our children—and not as much on getting positive "results" through conflict resolution. Arguments and fighting do have positive outcomes in that our children learn to handle conflict and also learn about themselves and their hearts in the process. Conflict between siblings can bring about a good and sanctifying work in our children if we take care to guide them in their interactions and relationship development as outlined in this book. We want our homes to be places marked by encouragement and grace, forgiveness and repentance, so let's be thoughtful in how we approach our children with the ideas discussed within these pages.

Overall, our goal is to guide our children from sibling rivalry to family harmony. The main tool for us to do that is to truly love our kids. Love them when they're fighting. Love them when they're at peace. Love them individually. Love them as a group. Love them most of all for who they are at this moment.

We should demonstrate that love to them in a thousand little ways throughout our lives. As we love them, we can help them work on moving from war to peace—and from there, to a more healthy and happy relationship with each other. The task ahead might seem daunting, but keep in mind that by making even small changes, you can redirect the tone in your home from friction to one that is more loving, kinder, and more welcoming to those who reside there.

Notes

Introduction

1. Some who responded to my survey and interview requests declined to give their full names, while others asked me to use an alias.

2. Jane Mersky Leder, *Brothers & Sisters: How They Shape Our Lives* (New York: Ballantine Books, 1991), 34.

3. Jane Mersky Leder. "Adult Sibling Rivalry," psychologytoday.com, January 1, 1993, http://www.psychologytoday.com/articles/199301/adult-sibling-rivalry, accessed January 3, 2014.

4. S. McGuire, S. M. McHale, and K. Updegraff, "Children's perceptions of the sibling relationship in middle childhood: Connections within and between family relationships," *Personal Relationships* 3 (1996): 229-39.

5. Jeffrey Kluger, "The New Science of Siblings," time.com, July 10, 2006, http://content.time.com/time/magazine/article/0,9171,1209949,00.html, accessed January 3, 2014.

6. Jeffrey Kluger, *The Sibling Effect: What the Bonds Among Brothers and Sisters Reveal About Us* (New York: Riverhead Books, 2011), 41.

7. Frank Bruni, "The Gift of Siblings," nytimes.com, May 25, 2013, http://www.nytimes.com/2013/05/26/opinion/sunday/bruni-the-gift-of-siblings.html?_r=0, accessed January 3, 2014.

Chapter 1

1. George Howe Colt, "Sibling Rivalry: One Long Food Fight," nytimes.com, November 25, 2012, http://www.nytimes.com/2012/11/25/opinion/sunday/sibling-rivalry-one-long-food-fight.html?pagewanted=1&_r=0, accessed November 11, 2013.

2. Kluger, *The Sibling Effect*, 9-10.

Chapter 2

1. Judy Barrett, "How to Raise Children with a Servant's Heart," judybarrettblog (blog), http://judybarrettblog.com/2012/11/08/how-to-raise-children-with-a-servants-heart/, accessed January 10, 2014.

2. Ibid.

Chapter 3

1. Monica Brady-Myerov, "After 35 Years, 'Car Talk' Brothers Retiring," wbur.org, June 8, 2012, http://www.wbur.org/2012/06/08/car-talk, accessed January 29, 2014.

2. Rachel Pomerance, "Harbaugh Brothers: A Healthy Sibling Rivalry?" usnews.com, February 4, 2013, http://health.usnews.com/health-news/articles/2013/02/04/harbaugh-brothers-a-healthy-sibling-rivalry, accessed November 27, 2013.

Chapter 4

1. Kluger, *The Sibling Effect*, 87-88.

2. Jill J. Suitor, et al., "Within-Family Differences in Parent-Child Relations Across the Life Course," *Current Directions in Psychological Science* 17, no. 5 (October 2008): 334-38.

3. S. T. Williams, K. J. Conger, and S. A. Blozis, "The development of interpersonal aggression during adolescence: The importance of parents, siblings, and family economics," *Child Development* 78 (2007): 1526-42.

4. Pomerance, "Harbaugh Brothers: A Healthy Sibling Rivalry?"

5. Kluger, *The Sibling Effect*, 69.

6. John Rosemond, "High self-esteem for kids a sham," washingtontimes.com, April 12, 2009, http://www.washingtontimes.com/news/2009/apr/12/rosemond-high-self-esteem-for-kids-a-sham/, accessed May 16, 2014.

7. Ibid.

Chapter 5

1. Kluger, *The Sibling Effect*, 44.

2. Melody Spier, "How to Treat Your Different Children Fairly," Raising Small Souls (blog), http://raisingsmallsouls.com/how-to-treat-your-different-children-fairly/, accessed December 6, 2013.

Chapter 6

1. Kellie "Red," "The Gift of Siblings," Building Cathedrals (blog), patheos.com, August 8, 2013, http://www.patheos.com/blogs/building cathedrals/2013/08/the-gift-of-siblings/, accessed January 29, 2014.

2. Susan Alexander Yates, personal correspondence.

3. Kluger, *The Sibling Effect*, 13.

Chapter 7

1. John Rosemond, *The Well-Behaved Child* (Nashville: Thomas Nelson, 2009), 140.

Chapter 8

1. William West, "One-on-one time with parents is crucial," Family Edge (blog), mercatornet.com, December 10, 2012, http://www.mercatornet.com/family_edge/view/11584, accessed December 21, 2013.

Chapter 10

1. Kluger, *The Sibling Effect*, 133.

Conclusion

1. Kluger, *The Sibling Effect*, 272-73.

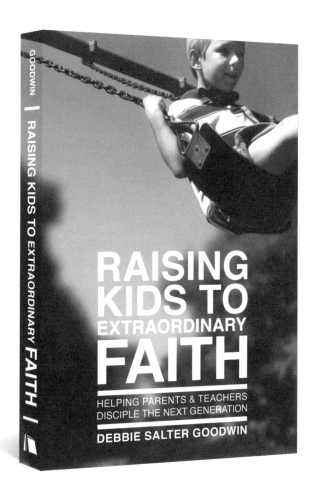

We want our children to know and love Jesus and learn what it means to be His disciple.

Filled with spiritual growth ideas and suggestions for developing faith-enriched homes and church environments, *Raising Kids to Extraordinary Faith* offers purposeful advice, spiritual insight, and essential awareness to help parents and ministry workers make discipleship the key component of their guidance.

Raising Kids to Extraordinary Faith
ISBN 978-0-8341-2391-5

BEACON HILL PRESS
OF KANSAS CITY
www.BeaconHillBooks.com

Teach Your Children to Love Like Jesus

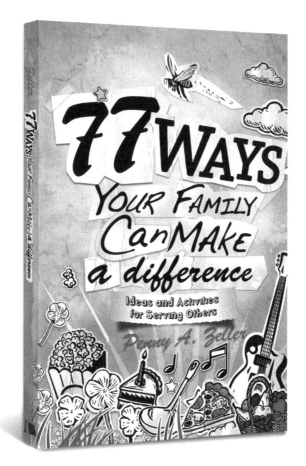

Serving others—loving them the way we love ourselves—is the heartbeat of the Christian faith. Packed with 77 suggestions and activities designed to serve the needs of people in your community, this fun and insightful book will help you cultivate love and compassion in your kids as you discover ways your family can make the world a better place by impacting the lives of others.

77 Ways Your Family Can Make a Difference
ISBN 978-0-8341-2370-0

BEACON HILL PRESS
OF KANSAS CITY

www.BeaconHillBooks.com